living with equals

living with equals

JERRY KLASMAN

An Individualist's Guide to Emotional and Romantic Happiness

Delacorte Press / Eleanor Friede • New York

Manufactured in the United States of America
First printing

Library of Congress Cataloging in Publication Data

Klasman, Jerry, 1928–
Living with equals.

Bibliography: p.
Includes index.
1. Marriage.   2. Interpersonal relations.
3. Equality.   I. Title.
HQ734.K614   301.41   75-17785
ISBN 0-440-05560-1

To Edith Efron

contents

PRELUDE   ix

THE CROSSROADS: Myth vs. Reality   1

SOVEREIGNTY OR SLAVERY:
You Can't Have It Both Ways   15

JEALOUSY: Distortions and Injustice   30

EMOTIONS, VALUES, AND HIERARCHIES:
You Are What You Value   47

LOVE   74

MONOPOLIES: Coercive and Natural   87

LIVING WITH EQUALS:
To Be Free You Must Offer Freedom   105

GLOSSARY   131
ACKNOWLEDGMENTS   135
BIBLIOGRAPHY   137
INDEX   139

prelude

In a vague and uncertain way, some of the concepts underlying *Living With Equals* first occurred to me twenty-five years ago. That was near the beginning of "togetherness": the period after World War II when The Myth of two lives becoming one, a split-level with patio, and clearly drawn sex roles—wife/mother at home taking care of the children and the split-level, husband/father on the job and involved in Little League and the Scouts—was in full flower.

There was no feminist movement then, no civil rights movement either. American consciousness was domestic, patriarchal, and inward-looking. (Despite an emerging new consciousness in the land, it still is that way to a marked degree.)

For reasons of my own life situation rather than philosophy, I had impulses in a different direction. Caught up in the spirit of the times, I was nonetheless bothered. In the end I ignored the troublesome impulses and began a romantic career as a round peg in a square hole. I took what solace I could from the fact that almost everyone I knew was in the same boat.

The ignored ideas wouldn't stay ignored, however, and four or five years ago I began working on them in earnest. In the process a curious truth about myself bobbed to the surface. I had enjoyed a few relationships with men that had been subjected to great strain and survived, whereas my romantic relationships had collapsed under the same, or even less stressful, conditions. Why?

Logic told me that I was either picking on the wrong sex for my romances, or I was doing something wrong in my romantic life that I wasn't doing wrong in my fraternal life. (I rejected offhand the possibility that you can't be equally successful in both.)

Dismissing the wrong-sex theory on the basis of gut reaction, I addressed the other question: What was I doing right in my fraternal relationships that I wasn't doing right in my romantic relationships? The answer was not too hard to find. My long-lasting relationships with men had all been on an eyeball-to-eyeball basis. A feeling of absolute and unyielding peer-ness pervaded them. We were equals.

The obvious next question was: Could I say the same

about my romantic relationships? The answer was a dismaying NO!

I began to think about my own relationships, about the relationships of others I knew, and about the relationships of anyone who was willing to discuss them with me. My understanding began to grow. I organized my thoughts into a series of lectures. I learned from those lectures that, to one extent or another, most of my audiences had similar problems, and more than a few had come up with similar solutions.

I cemented old and new friendships in those lectures— and I lost a couple as well. Both experiences lead me to believe that *Living With Equals* is on the right track.

I offer these ideas as a starting point. They've worked for me and for others, but they need to be homogenized into your own life before they'll do you any good. They're a bare outline waiting for you to give them shape and substance.

JERRY KLASMAN
January 1975

living with equals

the crossroads
MYTH VS. REALITY

"There was a period in my life when I dated 'slick' guys, Don Juans. It was strictly a kind of social prejudice on my part. I wanted to capture the most attractive man in the room. They were the only kind of men I wanted to be with."

Mary, a very together lady these days, was telling me about one of her former destructive romance patterns.

"It was a foolish pattern," she continued, "a very painful pattern because, though I was attracted to their Don Juan-ism, I knew they had no real standards. Especially in sex. I never could trust them. There was never a really deep emotional relationship with any of them. I knew what they were. I *knew* they were shallow bastards who laid anybody they could get their hands on. *I knew it!* I had to figure that if they weren't with me they were in bed with *some*body and it really didn't make any difference to them whose body it was.

"Yes, those were very destructive relationships. For example, any time one of them came to my house I felt I had to look letter-perfect. I had to be their perfect mate. I dieted and exercised; set my hair constantly and, you know, I was really tied up in the way I looked all the time. It was a very self-destructive kind of thing. A bad habit. I don't recommend that pattern to anyone."

She continued, "When I was much younger, I sometimes confused platonic love or friendship with romantic love. Like believing you're in love with the boy next door who's been like a brother."

Mary paused. "I married one," she said.

"I was raised a strict Catholic," Phil said. "I got married when I was thirty-three to a very good Catholic girl and we lived up to the rules of the Catholic church very rigorously. But, as you try to lead this Christian life where two people become one, it causes conflicts in a person who considers himself sovereign and independent.

"I owned my own business and I had been attempting to put into practice the liberal-type education I had and make money and I discovered that *that* didn't work. So, I had to change my views on economics quickly. That was my introduction to Ayn Rand, her book *Capitalism: The Unknown Ideal.* In the introduction Rand suggests you first read the essays on 'Man's Rights' and 'The Nature of Government' in the Appendix. I read them—it takes maybe twenty or thirty minutes?—and I said, 'Hey, there goes my wife, my family, my religion, my business. My whole life is *changed.*'

"At that point I began to work toward getting out of the set of circumstances I was in. I attempted to enlighten my wife so she could join me in what I had discovered to be true about the proper way to live, but she wouldn't have anything to do with it. There was no coping with the situation because she was not philosophically inclined to those ideas, so we just kept growing further and further apart.

"She took harbor with her family, and I knew I was going to alienate not only my wife, but my parents, brothers, and sisters, but I knew it had to be done. You only live once."

"Well," Lee said, "I was married once. I had mixed feelings about it, but the whole thing was decided on the spur of the moment. It only took three days to get everything together and we were ready to go.

"My mother never discouraged me in anything I wanted to do so I never really felt that she didn't like the idea. When we talked about it she just asked if I was thinking and paying attention to what I was doing. I told her why

I had agreed to marry Neal and she said, 'Well, I see you've given it some thought so it's all right.'

"Just before the ceremony, I said to my father, 'Dad, I can't do it. I've thought and thought about it and it's wrong, morally wrong. I don't even know him that well. Please do something.' Well, my father said I had to do it because I had *promised*.

"He grabbed me, literally, and dragged me, really dragged me down the aisle. My mother's eyes were staring! Later she asked me what the problem was and I told her I hadn't wanted to go on with it. She said, 'Why didn't you tell me? I would have married him! Anything to have stopped it!'

"I've never quite forgiven myself for that. I could very easily have turned on my heel and walked away and no one would have said anything, as I've since found out. No one would have said BOO! But at the time I thought, well, my father *said* I had to go through with it so I guess it's right.

"He was wrong. I could have done anything and Neal would have said 'Fine.' I still feel guilty about it all in some respects because backing out then would have made things a lot more pleasant for many people, including myself.

"Six months later, it was over. I had the marriage annulled."

*   *   *

"You see, I was afraid of giving up my independence."

David went on, "I was afraid of losing what I had developed as an individual and what I had found out about my life and life-style. I was *very* afraid of having someone take it from me and that fear meant I recognized that it was possible for me to give someone the permission to do so.

"I felt that whoever I married would usurp some of my independence. It might be by the 'salami' technique—a slice at a time. You don't miss a slice at a time, but eventually you'll find the whole salami is gone. The salami technique worked so well in those days that in my marriage I even questioned my right to go back to school at night to pursue my research.

"I know that now I have the greatest amount of freedom I've ever had. But, I still have to guard it."

Mary, Phil, Lee, and David, each in their own way, are describing the futility and unhappiness that comes from living your life by the standards of others. Mary fell for the "boy next door" myth and the "judge me by my conquests" fallacy. Phil had to face the prospect of alienating wife and family because of changing values. Lee gave in to pressures to do something against her better judgment. David was afraid of his vulnerability to the demands of others. All were handicapped to some degree by standards that were not their own.

We come into the world *tabula rasa,* a blank tablet. People, and through them institutions and traditions, then begin to write instructions on that tablet to educate us in human behavior. During our most impressionable years parents and society instruct us in the arts of living and loving. Definitions and ideals are handed down with all the certainty of the Delphic Oracle. Prescriptions for happiness are transmitted to our receptive minds and, as many struggling contemporary women will tell you, those prescriptions are often as incomprehensible as the prescriptions for antibiotics you get from your doctor.

At an age when we've no basis for comparison or experience to guide us, we're propelled into traditional romantic life-styles that are, for the most part, based on superstition, prejudice, and authoritarianism camouflaged as society's collective wisdom. Later, when we discover that these life-styles don't produce the happiness we've been led to expect, we're really up against it for an explanation. After all, a lot of "experience" went into developing these ideals, and if they don't work for us, the fault must be ours. Convinced that society's model of romantic happiness *will* work if we're "normal" and reasonably "healthy," we're apt to assume that we're not normal and a little unwell if it doesn't.

What is this rarely workable utopian model of romantic bliss? First and foremost it's a model that ignores far too much of what we learn through life experience. It promises constant peace and fulfillment without effort, but most of us know that anything that's achievable without effort, even peace and fulfillment, is of little value.

It promises an end to emotional uncertainty, striving, and loneliness, but only death can make that promise—and the profit isn't worth the cost.

It promises total sharing and mutuality of interest, but that could only (conceivably) be achieved by cloning.* It promises an ever-growing (or at least never-diminishing) passion for your lover and an end to emotional and sexual responses to anyone else. Experience shows us that the failure rate for those two promises is close to 100 percent.

Finally, there's the assurance that you'll enjoy all this emotional and romantic security without feeling hemmed in, without feeling a loss of independence or control; that you will, in fact, feel a profound freedom. Perhaps, but if so it will be the freedom of the heaven myth, with no striving and hence no accomplishment; there is only peace, joy, and happiness without end and without effort.

But these utopian promises are not often kept. There is something seriously wrong with an ideal of romantic happiness that fails to work for the vast majority. You wonder how the myth survives until you begin to pay close attention to exactly who still believes in it.

Try this experiment. From among your friends select a small number, half of them never married, if possible—and no newlyweds, please—and ask them if they expect

* The *exact duplication* of an organism through the use of that organism's own cells and genes.

7

to achieve the utopian romantic life-style I've described. I'll make only one prediction on the results: If you get any affirmative answers, you'll get more of them from the never-married.

Life experience is a great antidote for mythology!

After you've tried to live The Myth, perhaps several times, and recognize it for what it is, you're at the crossroads. Behind you stretches the road you've traveled thus far, and in front are three options. Straight ahead is a continuation of the past. That is *resignation*. You'll plunge ahead if you believe that the past predicts the future, and nothing you can do will change it.

To the left stretches the road of "adjustment." That choice requires you to redefine happiness in terms of what is possible within the prescriptions and prejudices you've learned. That means: Try to be satisfied—or at least not unhappy—with what occurs in your life, whatever it is. On this road you must "come to terms" with life and "abandon your foolish, childish, and *selfish*" demands for self-defined happiness.

This road is appealing because it is so well traveled. You'll never lack for company. There's lots of help in this direction: therapists, religions, concerned friends, all ready to help you on your way if you stumble or find the going a bit heavy. About the only thing you won't find is real living space, but then you won't really want it. You'll always need and often want the aid and example of fellow travelers who can help keep alive the dream of finding peace and happiness in the "what-is."

Your third option, if more-of-the-same or adjusting-to-the-what-is don't appeal to you, is to the right: the road to self-determination. Actually it isn't a road at all, it's only a direction. The road doesn't exist yet; you have to build it yourself. From your vantage point at the cross-roads you may not be able to see very far and that can be a little scary. But as soon as you choose your destination and begin the trip, you'll find you're not in a wilderness. Other people have been there before you; a lot of them.

Mary, Phil, Lee, and David are four of the road builders I've met. They are happier now than they've ever been, and their capacity to create happiness for themselves increases daily. They, and others like them, are self-motivated. Their happiness is self-defined. They've chosen their own destinations and are building their way toward them.

How do you build that road? What "material" do you use? I can't describe it in detail because it varies from person to person. After all, it's your road, not mine. But there are some materials that everyone must use.

The first is *sovereignty*. Control your own life. The destination must be of your own choosing.

The second is *values*. The "I wants." You must decide what you value, what you want; and you must refuse to let any person, institution, or tradition talk you out of pursuing what you want.

The third is *equality*, psychological equality. You must

respect and encourage the sovereignty of others as diligently as you do your own.

Choosing your own goals—sovereignty; choosing your own standards—values; recognizing the sovereignty of others—equality. That's the place to start.

Let's return to Mary, Phil, Lee, and David to see how well they're doing.

"There was a man I dated briefly," Mary said, "and he became extraordinarily serious very fast. He started talking marriage and I kept trying to avoid it because I wasn't the least bit interested. At one point he decided to corner me. His method was to take me to an elegant restaurant, order a very expensive meal including a bottle of Dom Perignon, and, as we were being served, say, 'Now! You must listen to what I am going to say. You can't leave.'

"Well, I picked up my purse and said, 'Hey, listen, fella, I walked away from four years of marriage. If you think I can't walk away from a prime rib, you're wrong.' And I grabbed a cab and went home. I left him among his two prime ribs, Caesar salad, and bottle of champagne and never saw him again."

"One day I saw this girl across a room with this look on her face," Phil said. "There was a real and alive person behind those eyes and an intellect that beamed. I said to myself, 'I've got to get out of this marriage I'm in. As long as I'm in it and committed to that one woman and that one relationship, if I ever meet a woman like *that* no relationship is possible.' Seeing that girl impressed on my mind that there were people out there like that, and if I was lucky enough to meet one of them—of course, I might not ever meet them, but it was a possibility—but if I did, under the conditions of my life at the time, very little could come of it because I had made a one-on-one commitment. I had given my word. I had a contract. So I went about finding mutual grounds for dissolving that contract."

Lee was talking about her marriage. "I couldn't play Susie Female twenty-four hours a day. I couldn't constantly walk around in a dress looking pretty and being sweet all the time. You see, you just can't do that lying down, you have to do it standing up, too, if someone sees you like that.

"There are times I want to curse or throw things; times I'd like to say, 'I hope you drop dead.' There are times when you really feel things other than being 'super-sweetheart.' When I realized my husband wanted me to dress up and be a 'Barbie' doll all the time, that's when I left."

"I'll give you a good example," David said. "These are the surroundings I am very comfortable with. I don't need more. I've chosen to live in what I call meager surroundings. It's not a hovel, and I can afford several times this, but I don't need a fancy apartment. I don't choose to spend my money that way. It's more important to me to spend my money on the theater, concerts, and the like. Those things are more of a value to me than where I live.

"Now I know that many women would have trouble living in these surroundings. That's an individual preference, and this apartment is *my* preference."

I'd say that Mary, Phil, Lee, and David are very definitely setting their own standards.

Setting your own standards, especially new ones associated with romantic attitudes and life-styles, isn't quite as simple as changing your shoes. First, the ideals you've grown up with are like Linus's blanket—you've always had them and can feel lost without them. Then, too, our society, with its vested interest in The Myth, can turn nasty if you show signs of ignoring its wisdom.

But the two biggest stumbling blocks for most people are (1) believing they CAN break the old habits that keep them from achieving an uniquely personal life-style; and (2) getting rid of the unconscious authoritarianism toward others that can frustrate that life-style if they do achieve it. The first problem requires understanding your own psychology. The second is the issue of living with equals.

Living with equals is mostly a matter of common sense. It means: Live your life solely by your own standards *and give unqualified approval to the idea of others doing the same*. It's a two-part proposition. First, you choose your values and live by them despite possible opposition from family, friends, society. Second, you recognize the *absolute right* of others to do the same even if the results are displeasing to you.

It's ironic that this two-parter is accepted intellectually by almost everyone, but few people actually live that way. This isn't just a failure of common sense; it's the result of basic contradictions in the things we've been taught. For example, we learn that independence and self-reliance are virtues. On the other hand, we learn that we all depend on others for happiness, that "no man is an island." With two such opposites rattling around in our heads, it's not hard to understand how people can believe in living by their own standards, but fail to do so in order to avoid the "desert island" effect.

In order to live with and as equals you need to reexamine the principles and prejudices you acquired when you were young. Central among these are your ideas about the nature of emotions, love, jealousy, sex and romantic life-styles. You also have to learn to recognize your own authoritarianism, even socially sanctioned kinds.

Here are several questions you may want to think about before reading any further. If you're curious enough, jot down your answers and, after finishing the book, answer the questions again. A comparison of the two sets of answers may prove to be very revealing.

1. Where do you think emotions come from? Can they be changed?
2. Is it possible to be entirely, psychologically independent of others?
3. Define *complete freedom*. Is it possible?
4. Define *romantic* (nonplatonic) *love*.
5. Are romantic love and independence compatible? Does love require compromise?
6. Can you be in love (nonplatonically) with more than one person at a time?
7. What is jealousy? Is it ever a positive emotion? Is everyone jealous sometimes?
8. Is marriage the ideal romantic life-style?

sovereignty or slavery
YOU CAN'T HAVE IT BOTH WAYS

"Do I really have a choice? I'm thirty-four years old, for chrissakes. The place to start is with the kids. They haven't picked up the defenses, the jealousy, the insecurities we have. I can't get those things out of my system now, they're too ingrained, too deep.

"Maybe it is all cultural, as you say, but it's too late for me to change. All I can do now is make the best of what I've got."

That is only one version of a statement I've heard countless times: "I can't change." Sometimes the blame is put on culture, sometimes on heredity or instinct or libido à la Freud, but the argument is always the same: "There's no real choice available. I'm stuck with being the way I am."

Of course, common sense and experience confirm that we do have a choice. If we don't, we're not self-responsible. "Responsibility" can apply only in a universe that includes choice. If we *must* do what we do, we have no control over the consequences; thus we have no responsibility.

You can't have it both ways.

The capacity to choose—will or volition—is part of our nature. Another word for that capacity is *sovereignty,* the general meaning of which is *original and independent authority or prerogative.* Authority over what? Over ourselves. Over what we do, think, or feel.

I define individual sovereignty as our independent prerogative to determine our own values, actions, goals, thoughts, and convictions.

You are sovereign. It is in the nature of things that you are sovereign. Your sovereignty is not a gift, not conditional, not negotiable. You are sovereign whether or not you exercise that sovereignty. Even the decision to accept the standards imposed on you from outside is a choice, an exercise of sovereignty.

We all exercise sovereignty, at least to some degree. The most dedicated conformists must, at some time and in some way, make choices on their own. Those who steadfastly deny the existence of individual sovereignty had to choose to hold that view.

The existence of sovereignty isn't merely a theoretical issue, it is fundamental to the achievement of happiness. To quote Nathaniel Branden, "Happiness is . . . the consequence of pursuing and achieving consistent, life-serving values."*

Sovereignty is required to decide which values are "life-serving," to be "consistent" in that decision, and to pursue those values as well as achieve them. Mary, Phil, Lee, and David exercised their sovereignty to choose, pursue, and achieve values that were, by their standards, "life-serving." Without that exercise of sovereignty they would still be in their former, unhappy circumstances.

Sovereignty is the basis of psychological freedom and self-determination. If you are without sovereignty—a state that is possible only through abdication—you have no control over your life. If you give up sovereignty, even willingly and out of love, to lovers, parents, or friends; even unconsciously, to tradition, society, or the commands of a duty you haven't consciously and freely accepted; even fearfully, to bosses, bullies, moralists, or demagogues—the resulting loss of control over your life will make you feel like a victim. That is the psychological fate of all slaves.

Sovereignty or slavery. You can't have it both ways.

* *The Psychology of Self-Esteem* (Los Angeles: Nash Publishing Corp., 1969), p. 251.

Love and fear are the two most apparent reasons for abdicating sovereignty, but they are not causes. The primary foe of sovereignty is *authoritarianism,* the doctrine of obedience to authority as opposed to individual liberty. The primary cause of abdication of sovereignty is the acceptance of authoritarian control.

Authoritarianism is part of our culture. Authoritarianism is some people telling the rest: "We have decided that thus-and-such is good for you and we've passed a law—or created a tradition or checked with God—and now you must obey." Never mind that, given a choice, you would do otherwise. They have decided what's best and that's the way it's going to be. Authoritarianism isn't concerned with individual liberty or sovereignty. It's concerned solely with obedience to whatever set of rules and standards it has decided to promote.

Our culture is sagging under the weight of authoritarian restrictions on our liberty. In many states, for example, males cannot adopt children, women may not refuse sex to their husbands, and consenting but unmarried adults may not have sex at all.

Children are particular targets of authoritarianism. For example, regardless of their ability to prove their responsibility, children may not obtain credit, petition the court on their own behalf (especially against their parents), or sign contracts. Adolescent sex is not only illegal, it is considered perverted. In many places businessmen may not open their stores on Sunday; people may not gamble, buy alcoholic beverages, use contraceptives, enter into cohabitational contracts that the state will recognize, marry someone of another race, and on and on and on.

Such prohibitions on our liberty are first a part of our culture and then a part of our law. The authority behind them is people organized into groups labeled government, religion, social clubs and country clubs, neighborhood associations and "private communities," unions and corporations, universities, political parties, and that indefinable, immeasurable, but somehow omnipotent thing called "the public." To the extent that we agree with or support these groups in their authoritarian attitudes we are authoritarian as individuals; we engage in, or support, efforts to prevent others from living their lives as they want to live them.

Sovereignty or slavery. You can't have it both ways.

If sovereignty is your independent prerogative to determine your own values, actions, goals, thoughts, and convictions, then clearly authoritarianism attempts to usurp that prerogative. Authoritarianism tells you what to value, how to act, what goals to choose, and what to think and believe. Authoritarianism opposes liberty and sovereignty; it attempts to dominate. That domination, when successful, results in control—control of the persons who are the targets of the authoritarianism. To the extent that your life is controlled by others, you are a slave.

You may not feel like a slave in an authoritarian society (depending on the society, of course) because, despite the number of choices you've lost, many may be retained.

This isn't to deny the loss of sovereignty when it occurs, or to minimize it, but simply to stress that people are able to focus on their remaining freedoms and ignore their slavery.

When authoritarian control exists on a person-to-person level, however, awareness of it rises. If the personal authoritarianism doesn't exceed the level of cultural authoritarianism, the resulting loss of control is still tolerable because it is consistent with the level of authoritarianism in the society. It all seems part of the same social fabric. But as the level of personal authoritarianism rises, and presuming awareness rises as well, the control begins to take on a different character. It begins to feel like exploitation. You begin to feel *owned* almost in the same sense as a piece of property is owned.

CONTROL MEANS OWNERSHIP

Personal authoritarian control is ownership.

If you're in control of a piece of property—a house, a car, a tennis racquet, a pair of shoes—you can decide what to do with that property. You can keep it, sell it, loan it, give it away, leave it out in the rain, wear it out, put it in a safe-deposit box. You have full authority, power, and dominion over it.

As I'll be using the term, *ownership is the power to control, define and/or inhibit the values, actions, goals, thoughts and convictions of another; the control of any*

20

or all aspects of another person's life. Anyone who seeks or exercises such control over others is really trying to own them.

On the surface, there are two ways for ownership to enter a romantic relationship. The first is through abdication of sovereignty, and the most common form of that is mutual abdication. This is inherent in the "voluntary" and mutual agreements promoted by The Myth and conventionally accepted by lovers, especially in marriage. When these agreements require an abdication of sovereignty, for example, when a wife accepts a role and gives up the profession she loves and prefers to keep in order to take care of the house for her husband (who agrees to become the sole provider), ownership is being exercised. It's irrelevant that the loss of sovereignty is voluntary. In situations where control exists—if the husband insists that the wife not go back to work—sovereignty is undercut and ownership is being exercised.

If a loss of sovereignty is called voluntary, it is either not a loss of sovereignty or not voluntary. It can't be both. If you give up something you want for something you want even more, you are not abdicating your sovereignty, you're exercising it. You are choosing the more important over the less important. However, if you give up something you want for something you want less, clearly you are making that choice for some reason other than your own priorities. That means you are under pressure or control from the outside; you are abdicating your sovereignty.

You can't have it both ways.

21

The other way of establishing ownership in a romantic relationship is through the coercion of emotional blackmail. Here's an example:

Pei is a quiet but very independent and outspoken person. She met Ben at a party and started dating him. "Ben acted like I was made of porcelain," Pei explained. "He was a big man. Not rough—intellectual, really—just large. In a couple of months we began sleeping together and that was very good except he seemed a little surprised to learn that I liked it so much. He knew I wasn't interested in marriage or even living with him, but he also knew I liked going to bed with him.

"About a year later he got transferred down south. We missed each other and I visited him once and he came to New York twice. About eight months after he moved he called me to say he'd quit his job and would be moving back to town in a month and asked if he could stay with me until he found a place to live. I was glad he was coming back, but I wasn't thrilled about his plan to move in. He'd mentioned marriage or living together often enough in the past to make me wary.

"I said okay though, and a month later he arrived. He found a job fast enough, but he wasn't working very hard on finding an apartment, and I told him so. That started it. First it was marriage and then it was shacking up. He was determined to convince me to do one or the other. When I finally got it through his head that I didn't intend to do either, he came apart at the seams. He started to drink a lot. I tried to talk things out with him, but if the talk lasted more than an hour he'd wind up in tears. By the end of the night he'd be an emotional basket case and I'd be furious and feeling like the Dragon Lady both at the same time.

"I just couldn't handle his weakness. I felt responsible. If I had told him to check into a hotel instead of moving in with me, I don't think things would have deteriorated.

"I let it go on for four months. It ended when he quit his job again, or maybe got fired for all I know, and started blaming me. I didn't even get mad. I just packed up his things while he sulked in the living room, and started carrying the bags out to the street. He followed me asking what I thought I was doing, but I didn't even answer. I just opened the front door and threw his stuff out on the sidewalk. I was really glad he thought I was made of porcelain then. I'm sure he would have liked to hit me."

Unlike the above example, emotional blackmail usually happens after a relationship has been "regularized" by marriage or an agreement to live together. The problems of dissolving a "permanent" relationship are great enough to make a certain level of emotional blackmail the lesser of two evils.

Emotional blackmail is obviously authoritarian because its intent is to accomplish something that wouldn't be accomplished by voluntary means. The simple fact of an attempt to coerce proves the existence of an ownership trip whether or not the attempt is successful.

Mutual abdication and emotional blackmail are the means by which ownership enters a romantic relationship; but in the end, attempts at ownership succeed only because the target makes a gift of control through abdication. This is clearly true in mutual abdication, but even emotional blackmail depends on the gift mechanism for success. Because it is in the nature of things that you are sovereign, the heaviest emotional blackmail will fail if you say, "No, I will not give in!"

SOVEREIGNTIES "IN CONFLICT"

Part of the road-building material mentioned in Chapter 1 was *equality*, respecting and encouraging the sovereignty of others as diligently as your own. You can't live with and as equals unless you accept in others those things you demand for yourself.

If you have trouble accepting your lover's sovereignty you're probably suffering from some unfulfilled expectations. That is, you expect your lover to be or act in certain ways, and when they* don't, you become dissatisfied. How you handle that dissatisfaction will determine whether or not you are attempting to establish

---

* Throughout, I will be using "they" to avoid the unbearably awkward and boring "he or she." This is admittedly incorrect, but I believe it makes for easier reading.

ownership. If your reaction is to demand or bring pressure or threaten, or to pout, sulk, or rave in order to get your lover to meet your expectation, you're on an ownership trip and that's all there is to it.

Equality in romantic relationships requires a meshing of sovereignties comparable to the meshing of gears in a machine. The teeth on each of two gears mesh and transmit energy that makes the machine move. Similarly, the values of two people mesh and make a relationship move. When some values of one lover are not matched in the other, the situation is like a gear with missing teeth; there's no meshing and no energy transmitted. This loss of energy doesn't mean the relationship must grind to a halt any more than a few missing gear teeth must cause a machine to break down.

Some relationships have more matching, energy-transmitting values than others; and equality in a romantic relationship recognizes the mismatches as well as the matches. Living with equals requires living with differences, accepting the realities of your lover's life even when they don't match yours. And of one reality you can always be sure: You and your lover are not identical.

Differences between lovers come in several different varieties. There are differences of experiences and viewpoint that can enlarge your awareness. They add excitement and discovery to your life and contribute to your expansion as a person. They are one of the greatest sources of happiness in a romantic relationship, an important factor in that great emotional "high" you experience when the relationship is going well. Part of that "high" is the experience of a "new life" opening up to you, new and different eyes through which to see the familiar and commonplace. These are *growth differences*.

At the opposite end of the scale are *terminal differences*. These differences make a romantic relationship impossible. If you value honesty and you discover that your lover is a liar and a cheat, your relationship is facing a terminal difference and isn't likely to survive. When terminal differences are discovered in a relationship, they are often the result of a basic change in one partner's outlook. Many feminist women have discovered terminal differences in their relationships as their own self-images changed. If their lovers or husbands haven't accepted their new self-awareness, many such women have had to conclude that they faced choosing between their new concepts of self and their relationships. Those who gave up their relationships were responding to the existence of terminal differences. Those who gave up their new self-awareness were abdicating their sovereignty.

Somewhere between growth differences and terminal differences will be found a third category, *corroding differences*. Corroding differences do their damage by eating away at a relationship over a period of time. These differences are the point of conflict in many battles over sovereignty; they are the origin of most unfulfilled expectations. Many are really growth differences made corrosive by our expectations and authoritarian attitudes. Others are, or should be, merely irrelevant to the success or failure of a romantic relationship.

*   *   *

Paul and Anita have been together almost two years. Paul is an engineer turned salesman whose job requires great attention to detail and follow-through. Anita is a grade school teacher. Their relationship is working well except in one respect: Paul procrastinates in dealing with his own nonprofessional problems and decisions, and Anita attends to such things as if they were life-or-death matters. Paul tends to let problems and decisions hang fire long enough for many of them to settle themselves or dissipate, and Anita is almost compulsive in her determination to "get things settled." Anita often thinks Paul's attitude is perverse since he behaves differently on his job. Paul can't understand Anita's compulsiveness since she is a patient and sympathetic teacher.

To the outside observer, Paul and Anita could each benefit from a little of the other's attitude. Less dawdling would reduce the snowballing of problems that plagues Paul from time to time, and Anita would benefit from relaxing a little. These personality differences are becoming corrosive. The resulting conflict stems from the expectations each has of the other.

If Paul and Anita would recognize (1) that their own expectations are not sufficient reason for the other to attempt a radical change of personality, (2) that wanting the other to make such a change and disapproving of the other's disinterest in doing so are both authoritarian attitudes, and (3) that they each have something to learn from the other, the differences between them that are corroding their relationship would become differences contributing to their growth.

There is another possibility. Either Paul or Anita could say, "I don't want to change you and impose my values and standards, I just don't want to live with the procrastination (or constant crisis). This problem is destroying my peace of mind and that is more important than this relationship. Good-bye."

For Paul and Anita, then, there are only two practical solutions consistent with the survival of both sovereignties. The first (and on the face of it, the more sensible) is to respect the other's sovereignty and turn the corroding differences into growth differences. Or, still respecting sovereignty, conclude that the differences are terminal and end the relationship.

Here's another example. Chuck is telling me about one of his standards.

"I hate makeup with a passion. A number of the women I've gone with like makeup and I don't know how to deal with that. They've put it on because they like it, it makes them feel better. They feel they're prettier for me or for other people and for themselves. I can understand that. They put it on and I dislike it. It makes them less attractive to me, but my saying I hate makeup is not the same as saying I hate them for putting it on. Being able to talk about it without feeling we're exerting power on each other, or that the other person will feel attacked, is the way to deal with it. It's still really there. We both still think about it, but it doesn't diminish the relationship. In some ways it might strengthen the relationship. Being able to talk about it, reaching an understanding of this separateness is really, really important."

Respecting your lover's sovereignty is the ONLY way to be sure that the relationship is built on voluntarism and freedom of choice rather than on the abdication of sovereignty, on ownership. Chuck, Paul, and Anita are aware of the differences plaguing their romantic relationships. If Paul and Anita can deal with their differences as effectively as Chuck does, they'll find their relationship enlarged rather than diminished by those differences. Differences between you and your lover can become an adventure in self-expansion. Habits are often restrictive. The differences between you and your lover can be a motivation for breaking out of habitual behavior and discovering new possibilities, new potentials, and new strengths in your relationship.

jealousy
DISTORTIONS AND INJUSTICE

Jealousy is an ownership trip, *the* ownership trip. It is the quintessence, the *ne plus ultra* of authoritarianism. It is also a word used for several emotions that have nothing to do with authoritarianism.

One day I was walking down the street with a woman I had known a short time, a woman I was very interested in. The previous evening she had been on a date with a recent ex-lover. I knew about the date, but I didn't know anything about the demise of the relationship, whether the split was because of a minor spat or because of more serious problems. My relationship with the woman was so new that I felt some concern. It was possible, for all I knew, that she and her ex-lover might patch things up and that might be the end of our blossoming relationship.

As we walked I asked her how the date went, if she'd enjoyed herself. Her answer made it clear that, although she had enjoyed seeing her friend, she would have preferred to spend the evening with me. Hearing this, I breathed an audible sigh of relief and told her about the concern I had felt. She turned to me with a big smile and said, "Aha! So you *do* feel jealous once in a while."

Her reaction illustrates a common confusion over what is and what isn't jealousy. Two distinctly different emotional responses are commonly and incorrectly considered to be the same, only differing in degree: jealousy and insecurity. Children learn what jealousy is supposed to be very early in their social experience, probably by the age of six or seven. Parents, other adults and other children observe the child behaving in certain ways and say, "Stop being jealous." This admonition always refers to certain kinds of behavior, and the child learns to associate *jealousy* with that behavior. Thereafter, any emotion that accompanies that behavior is understood to be jealousy. The emphasis on behavior is so strong that all attendant emotions get lumped together as a result. The confusion is prolonged into later childhood and adult life because in a given context, such as romance, the *psychosomatic* effect of both is so similar that they *feel* the same. Nevertheless, they are different emotions. Envy

31

is still another emotion that is sometimes confused with jealousy, but for different reasons.

In order to sort them out, let's begin with the most commonly understood of the three—envy.

Envy is the emotional response to the experience of recognizing values you desire and do not yet have. Commonly, this experience occurs when you see someone else achieve values that are identical or similar to those you desire—fame, fortune, professional recognition, and so forth. Envy is a reasonable and not unhealthy emotion. If a friend inherits a million dollars and retires to become a painter, it is perfectly reasonable for you to feel, "I envy your freedom to pursue your goals free from financial worry." You are not expressing a desire to deprive your friend of good fortune, you are merely expressing a desire to enjoy a similar benefit.

Envy is often confused with *covetousness,* the desire for *specific values* belonging to others, not similar ones. If you covet your friend's inheritance, you want to have it instead of it belonging to them. As we shall see, this is not jealousy either.

The next most commonly understood response—and most often confused with jealousy—is insecurity.

Insecurity is the emotional response to the experience of fearfulness over your ability to achieve or retain values you desire. Insecurity in a romantic context is almost always called jealousy. I find that somewhat strange because in other contexts insecurity is not misunderstood in that way. For example, if you're reflecting on your own personality and recognize that you're not very assertive, not inclined to push hard for the things you really want, not very confident that good things will happen for you, or stay with you for long, then you'll probably recognize that you're not very self-confident—you're insecure. I'd be surprised if you concluded that "jealous" is the proper description of your personality.

Insecurity is an internal state, a self-evaluation, a condition of self-esteem. It is an appraisal of your relationship to the "outside world," to reality. It has virtually nothing in common with jealousy, but we need to define jealousy so we can compare them side by side.

Jealousy is the emotional response to the loss, or threat of loss, of emotional property. Notice that, whereas envy and insecurity apply to all values, any kind of value, jealousy applies only to a specific value—emotional property.

What is *emotional property?* It is that over which you have, or believe you have, emotional control. Jealousy exists only in relation to other conscious entities capable of emotion, and that is an important distinction. You can envy your neighbor's Rolls-Royce. You can feel insecure about making the payments on your own Rolls-Royce. But, if you own a Rolls-Royce and someone steals it, jealousy isn't the emotion you'll experience.

Jealousy and insecurity do have one point in common—loss. The perception of the loss, however, and the nature of that which is lost, is different for each emotion. In insecurity, the loss is occasioned by your own inability to prevent it; it is an inner failing or inadequacy. And that which is lost is not experienced as something you own and to which you have full right and "title."

For example, here's Joan describing an attack of insecurity of the type often called jealousy:

"We began seeing each other on a strictly social basis because he was married. Then he decided to get a divorce and our romantic relationship began to develop. Suddenly he was free to find anybody. He was free to roam around and look. At that time I didn't perceive that as threatening. Then we began running into the same girl over and over. She had a lot of the physical attributes I had, and she knew everything about economics in which Michael is very interested. Plus she was very feminine in the classic sense. I really perceived her as threatening, and kept putting myself down for it. She was making heavy overtures toward Michael and I kept telling myself not to worry, but then he asked her for a date. What a threat! It was very painful to me because I thought I was going to lose him to her. It was an insecurity on my part.

"I wanted to tell him not to go on the date, but I restrained myself. I told myself that if I was going to lose him, I could lose him over lunch; it didn't have to be a date with someone else that did it."

* * *

JEALOUSY: DISTORTIONS AND INJUSTICE

Joan was suffering from insecurity. Her fear of losing Michael's affection was the result of doubting her importance to him. In contrast, here's Lee relating an instance of real jealousy:

"There was a man that I was very fond of and we were at a party. There was a married woman who always physically chased my friend around. He had disappeared and when I found him there was this lady grabbing at him, pawing at him, and he obviously wasn't resisting. I had a twinge of jealousy because I knew that if I did the same thing he would have been horrified at me. I was totally out of control and had to walk away and get my thoughts together. It was a really strong feeling of being personally attacked.

"She had a privilege I didn't have. I was restricted as to when and where I could do certain things and I was extremely jealous that she was allowed to approach him physically in a way I was not. I felt I had been deprived, not only by that woman, but by the man also, of a certain kind of freedom that I would have liked to have with him. She was taking affection that I wanted, or that he could have given to me."

Ownership is the key to understanding jealousy. The experience of having proprietary attitudes toward your lover distorts your perception of certain events and promotes behavior we recognize as jealousy. I call this distorted perception the *poacher/predator mentality*.

The distortion is based on your belief that you have the right to control your lover's emotions and actions, as if they were your property. You claim sole use of, and benefit from, that property. Romantically, this claim refers to the emotions and sexuality of your lover and to a lesser degree, even their time and attention. If anyone "uses" your property without your permission; if anyone gains any emotional or sexual value, or even time and attention from your lover, you'll regard that person as a *poacher,* a thief. Thinking of your lover as property distorts your perception of the people and events in your lover's life.

Of the many distortions caused by the poacher/predator mentality the worst of the lot almost defies polite description. I refer to the attitude that if your lover engages in sex with anyone but you, their genitals become *dirtied, defiled.*

I realize that this attitude began centuries ago in an age when venereal disease was epidemic and incurable. But the view persists today *not* in hygienic terms, but in *moral* terms. I sense that although the cult of virginity is in rapid decline and only a small percentage of people concern themselves with their lover's prior sexual history, the discovery that their lovers had sex elsewhere *yesterday* causes a considerable percentage to react as if the organs employed were no longer fit for human use—like rotten eggplant.

It's so terribly sad, so *dehumanizing,* to think of one's lover only as a penis or vagina.

Because you believe that your lover's emotions, sexual capacity, time, and attention are subject to theft, you'll also suffer yet another distortion: You'll see the world as populated by *predators* who are poised to swoop down and carry off your romantic property. People cease to be just people, jobs just jobs, hobbies or other interests just forms of recreation; they all become threats to the "safety" of your property, and hence to you.

A third distortion will be in your perception of your lover. Your conviction that theft is possible can't be sustained unless you're also convinced that your lover is helpless, is incapable of resisting the attacks of the predators. This distortion may pump up your pseudo-ego by casting you in the role of protector, but it destroys your perception of your lover as an independent, self-determined person with values and standards. (That is, if such a perception survived your ownership trip that made all the distortions possible in the first place.)

Lee's experience illustrates all three distortions. The married woman was a poacher on her romantic property and a predator threatening her safety. Also, it is clear that she saw her friend as unable to resist the woman's advances. She did indeed fail to see him as an independent person with values and standards of his own (which, perhaps, she would have disagreed with).

This last distortion has another harmful effect. If you believe your lover is powerless to resist the predator, you must be aware, even dimly, that your lover was equally helpless in relation to you. That means: Your relationship isn't built on your lover's *choice* of you, but on your successful predation of their emotions. How does *that* make you feel?

Jealousy, then, is based on ownership and three distortions produced by ownership: seeing the people and events in your lover's life as poachers; seeing the world as populated by predators; and seeing your lover as a helpless pawn to both.

This bizarre view of your lover and the world (and jealousy, no matter how common, is nothing if not bizarre) can be said to have two components: *theft* and *siege*. It's important to understand them because they'll help you distinguish between insecurity and jealousy in yourself and others, and guide you in determining which problem you're facing. Of even greater value is the insight you'll gain about the workings of your own jealousy.

The theft component suggests that jealousy is accompanied by feelings of injustice, and in my experience that is the case. If you believe someone has *stolen* your lover's affection or time, a part of your jealous reaction will be to the *unfairness* of it all. You'll feel things like, "Why don't they go after someone who isn't already involved?" or "Why did they have to pick on *my* lover?" or "Why did my lover have to have someone else? Wasn't I enough?" These are expressions of the feeling that an injustice has been done; a feeling that you *deserve* better treatment than you've received and that is a clue to your ownership trip.

The siege component's implied evaluation of your lover as helpless triggers a backlash. Think back to the last time your lover had an attack of jealousy and you'll probably remember having one or more of the following reactions:

1. You were being unjustly accused of wrongdoing; you were being manipulated into accepting guilt.
2. Your lover had no confidence in you.
3. Your lover had no respect for your sense of right and wrong.
4. Your lover was being unfair or vicious toward whoever or whatever prompted the attack.
5. Your lover was attacking your autonomy.

Any or all of the above reactions can be expected if your attitude is that your lover is constantly under attack, invites attack either openly or covertly, and is incapable of resisting these attacks. In other words, this attitude declares: "People are always chasing you, you even encourage them, and you haven't the moral fiber to resist them." That's a heavy accusation to lay on someone you profess to love, but it is the message of the siege component of jealousy.

There is no room in an equal relationship for the poacher /predator mentality. Every aspect of this bizarre attitude is authoritarian and anti-sovereignty. In an equal relationship all you can expect from your lover is that which they are prepared to give as a sovereign person. Your expectations aren't obligations your lover must meet. Certainly, if your lover doesn't give you enough (by your standards) you, as a sovereign person, may decide that you require more and, if the difference is terminal, end the relationship. That reasoning is not the same as feeling like a victim of injustice. You'll never judge your lovers as unfair if you recognize that their sovereignty is as important to them as yours is to you.

Nor can an equal relationship withstand the implications of the siege component. If those implications happen to be true, if your lover (1) is a wrongdoer, that is, committed to acts that are harmful to you; (2) isn't worthy of your confidence; (3) is without a sense of right and wrong; (4) has friends, family, etc., who are a threat to your well-being; and (5) isn't competent to exercise autonomy; then you can't have an equal relationship in the first place. (If those things are true of you both, the relationship still won't be equal because of all the pathology—emotional disturbance—present.)

Have you ever wondered why certain emotional states—jealousy or aggression, for example—are said to be unavoidable and universal aspects of the human condition, whereas other states—insecurity or anxiety, for example—are not? I believe the explanation for this kind of silliness is traceable to the functions of these various emotional states in society. Anxiety and insecurity are disabling; they lower the "performance" level of those who are afflicted. Society wants a cure for this disability. Therefore, the "illnesses" aren't looked upon as incurable.

On the other hand, jealousy and aggression serve society in one way or another. They're "productive" to the extent that they further society's aims. Properly controlled jealousy helps in the regulation of sexual behavior and properly controlled aggression can be channeled into "good" works ranging from exploration and settlement, as in the American West, to the fighting of wars. Therefore, they're not considered "illnesses"; they're said to be universal characteristics of the species. That is, they are "natural," "normal," even "instinctive."

None of this makes sense. If insecurity and anxiety are curable illnesses, so are jealousy and aggression. Because not *everyone* is jealous or aggressive any more than *everyone* is insecure or anxiety-ridden. Take Phil, for example:

"I have never experienced jealousy in my whole life. People say they're jealous and I've dated women who were jealous and I do *not* know what that means. In the past I've thought, 'What's wrong with me? I never get jealous.' Hell, wars are fought and whole nations fall because of jealousy and I've never experienced that emotion.

"I think jealousy has to do with theoretical ownership and I don't think I own anybody and therefore don't have that emotion."

* * *

To the extent that jealousy is seen to play a "productive" role in society it gains social approval. In fact, it isn't uncommon to hear people boast of their lovers' jealousy. Such people appear to take pride in being objects of jealousy, as if that jealousy is a measure of their own worth.

On the other hand, since jealousy carried to its logical conclusion is "unproductive"—resulting in murder and mayhem—it earns disapproval as well. This ambivalence is apparent in the things we say about jealousy. For example: "A little jealousy proves that you love someone." But, "He was *too* jealous to suit me. I never gave him any cause for jealousy." But, "It was a crime of passion. After all, she caught him in bed with another woman."

Jealous homicide *is* a crime, but not without some sympathy. Given provocation, jealousy is considered acceptable if its expression is kept within bounds. But even when it is expressed too freely or strongly, it is regarded with some residual tolerance.

The acceptance of jealousy as a "natural" emotion colors most advice about dealing with it. Too often we are urged to accept our jealousies more or less uncritically, to concentrate on not acting them out, to live with the realization that jealousy can't be avoided but can be ignored or overridden. Such advice is mischievous even when it is helpful.

You don't *have* to live with jealousy! By all means resolve not to act on it, but that treatment alone is no more than a palliative. The cure will be found in giving up the idea that jealousy is natural and giving up the authoritarian attitudes that support it.

The first battle is to recognize your own impulses to exercise ownership. If you experience jealousy, ownership trips are there. Think about the poacher/predator mentality. To what extent and in what particular ways do you feel the claim to sole use and control of your lover's emotions, affections, and time? In what respects would your lover have to abdicate sovereignty in order to avoid doing things that trigger your jealousy? If you have ever been on the receiving end of a jealous attack, recall the sense of injustice you felt and ask yourself if you are doing the same thing to your lover.

Do you feel under attack from romantic "predators"? Do you view your lover's friends, family, job, and pastimes as poachers on your private domain? Do you feel cheated—really cheated—if someone else experiences any emotional or sexual contact with your lover?

Do you feel that you "deserve" better treatment than you're getting from your lover? Do you think your lover is incapable of discerning what is good or bad for them? (And do you think that question is irrelevant; that they should only be concerned with what is good or bad for you?)

Would you accept, without ANY reservations or exceptions, the same standards and limitations your jealousy would like to impose on your lover?

Only after learning to recognize your own authoritarianism will the determination not to act on jealousy be anything more than a cosmetic. And if you are fighting those first two battles, you won't be harsh with yourself when (or if) jealousy does strike. After all, you can't reverse the habits of a lifetime overnight. And you shouldn't expect to. In fact, if you have begun to recognize and understand emotional ownership, the occurrence of jealous feelings can be turned into a plus. Because jealousy is a *measure* of your authoritarianism and involvement in ownership, it provides a means for measuring your progress out of it. As you begin to notice a reduction in the frequency and intensity of your jealous attacks, you'll realize that your authoritarianism is also on the decline. The effect is much like successful dieting; the more fat (and authoritarianism) you lose, the better your self-image and the stronger your motivation becomes to lose it all!

One last word of caution. Openness is very important in any romantic relationship, and even more important when jealousy is a factor. If you are working to rid yourself of authoritarian feelings, the task will be easier if you let your lover know about it. Remember, your lover probably knows more about your authoritarian attitudes than you do, at least in the beginning. So don't struggle in secret and in silence.

On the other hand, don't use openness as a weapon. I've seen people make a big thing out of being open, but it was just a cover for sending their messages of jealousy. Here's an example:

Jenny and Carl have had a relationship for about a year. Carl owns his own business and is married. Jenny is single. She told me about a fight she and Carl had. The day of the fight, Carl had told his wife that he would be home late because of a conference on a project he was trying to sell. In fact, he expected to finish much earlier and planned to spend the evening with Jenny. Actually he didn't go into the office at all, and he and Jenny spent the whole day together.

About four o'clock that afternoon, one of Carl's employees, not knowing where the boss was, called Carl's home and left word that the evening meeting was canceled. Later, Carl called his office, learned about the call to his home, and called home himself. He gave his wife some kind of explanation about not being in the office and said that since the evening meeting had been canceled, he would be home shortly.

When Jenny heard that their plans were washed out she became very angry. "With your job you could be anywhere tonight," she snapped at Carl. "Just because that deal is off doesn't mean there aren't fifty others. How come you didn't get yourself together and explain where you were going to be tonight?"

Carl just shrugged and said, "We had the whole day. Don't be an ingrate."

"I don't care about the whole day," Jenny exploded. "She gets all the protection and you fit me in when you don't have to worry about what she thinks or feels. What about what I think or feel? I know you've got things to do at home but I want our time together and *I want to feel good about it. I don't want to worry about sneaking around and wondering whether the alibi will hold up.*"

At this point in the story, Jenny just shook her head a little and said, "All the goodness of that day was negated by how ugly it had become."

Now, there's no question about the real issue being Jenny's jealousy. She clearly expressed a feeling of injustice. But, after sending that message to Carl, she claimed to be upset about the sneaking around. She could have talked that over with Carl at any time because their relationship is an open one. In this instance, she tried to use openness to cover her attack of jealousy. Sneaking around and alibis weren't what provoked the attack; it was provoked by Carl's choice to go home since he and Jenny had been together all day.

Of course you should be open with your lover. Resentments, petty or important, will never dissipate otherwise. But be on guard. If you air a resentment at a time when it may interfere with your lover's sovereignty, or perhaps inflict guilt over the unavoidable, check your motives. On the other hand, if you delay discussion until a time when your resentment can't possibly inflict guilt or affect your lover's decision, you'll always be sure that you're using openness for constructive rather than destructive purposes.

emotions, values, and hierarchies

YOU ARE WHAT YOU VALUE

My friend Bob subscribes to the theory that high up in the Himalayas there is a group of monks who control, in every respect, the fates and fortunes of us lesser mortals down below. It seems these monks have a fantastic computer that keeps track of us, and the goal of it is to tantalize us with the prospect of success and then to dash our hopes with disappointment.

Thus, every time something good happens to Bob, he'll mumble, "I wonder what disaster those damn monks are setting me up for *this* time?"

Well, I doubt that many people believe they are the pawns of a group of technocratic lamas, but many do believe they're controlled by another kind of mysterious force—emotions. Countless times I've heard the claim that we're slaves to our emotions. Just as often I've heard people say we should come to terms with our emotions just as we should come to terms with an unpleasant boss or unpleasant weather or the unpleasant aspects of a lover's personality. This advice assumes that our emotions, like the weather or the personalities of bosses, lovers, and friends, are facts of life beyond our control, that the most we can hope for is some kind of peaceful coexistence. Much of present-day psychology seems bent on convincing us we have little or no control over our emotions and we are just a tantrum away from slipping back into savagery.

But emotions aren't mysterious, uncontrollable, or irrational. If we're victimized by our emotions it's because we don't understand them and how they came to be what they are. Emotions are self-created. We may create them in a purposeful, integrated, and consistent way or in a random, disintegrated, and inconsistent way. The former produces emotional stability; the latter, carried to the extreme, produces neurosis.

EMOTIONS

Emotions perform vital functions. They are our "radar," subconsciously evaluating the world around us when we haven't enough time or data to do it consciously. (Feeling "good vibes" or "bad vibes" are examples of the blips recorded by our emotional radar scanner.) Emotions warn us of danger. They are the means of experiencing happiness. They are the thermometer we use to diagnose the general health of our lives.

Love, affection, joy, fear, hate, sorrow, and the like, are *emotions*. They are expressions of values and value judgments. "An emotion is the psychosomatic form in which man experiences his estimate of the beneficial or harmful relationship of some aspect of reality to himself."* Or as Aristotle put it: Emotional pleasure or pain is in relation to the *good* or *bad* as such.

Good and *bad* are value judgments. You can test this for yourself through introspection. Think of the things you like: your lover, your children, your job, sunsets, a favorite painting or book—whatever pleases you. Do you feel a happy emotion? Of course. Because the things you've been thinking about are values and you know they're good-for-you, that is, good for your life. Thinking about things you dislike will produce the opposite effect because those things are *dis*values.

This simple analysis is all that nonscientists need to know. We experience emotion and that emotion refers to some person, thing, situation, idea, fantasy, expectation, etc., we know, or think we know, something about.

Here's a classic example of the proposition: Imagine that you aren't aware of the concepts *gun* or *firearm*. Imagine further that you don't have in your conscious or unconscious mind whatever concepts or images you now have

* Nathaniel Branden, *The Psychology of Self-Esteem* (Los Angeles: Nash Publishing Corp., 1969).

concerning the appearance or behavior of unstable, violent people. Now, imagine you're at a party and into the room walks a person who is brandishing a shotgun and acting in an unstable and potentially violent way without threatening you specifically. Whatever you might experience—curiosity about the object in his hands, for example—you wouldn't experience the emotion of *fear* because you'd have no way of knowing that his behavior is threatening or the object in his hand is dangerous.

In real life, of course, you'd instantly and without conscious thought be aware that the situation posed a threat to you. You'd make the value judgment that the situation was *bad* for you, and your emotional response would be fear or caution.

This is how perception becomes emotion. You perceive an object or idea and make an automatic value judgment, the meaning of which is either *good-for-me* or *bad-for-me*. You make the judgment without conscious thought, and it triggers various physical changes which you experience as emotion.

This explains the similarity of experience produced by jealousy and insecurity. If you see your lover kissing a romantic rival, insecurity may produce an appraisal of potential loss of your lover's affection, and your value judgment will be *bad-for-me*. Or, jealousy may produce the same appraisal and the same value judgment. Since in either case there is a *bad-for-me* value judgment associated with the loss, the physical changes experienced as emotions will be similar. Because the total experience of each emotion is different and that difference is dis-

cernible through introspection, and because the origins
of the emotions are different, they must be considered
different emotions.

VALUES

In order to make a value judgment you must have *values*.
If your life wasn't a value you wouldn't make the value
judgment that produces *fear* when threatened by a mad-
man with a gun.

A value is something that we believe to be desirable,
that is, good-for-us. Ayn Rand said it simply, "A 'value'
is that which one acts to gain and/or keep."*

However, believing that something is desirable and acting
to gain or keep it aren't automatic assurances that the
something is, in fact, good for you. Sovereignty means
that you have the power to choose, but it doesn't guaran-
tee that you'll choose that which is objectively good for
your life. Heroin addicts, for example, believe that a fix
is a value, is good for them, although heroin is a deadly
substance. Setting aside the question of the degree to
which their sovereignty is impaired by their addiction, to
addicts, fixes are values even though they are destructive
and antisurvival.

We must keep in mind that the freedom to choose our
own values also includes the freedom to choose values
that are destructive. But, whether our choices are con-

* *The Virtue of Selfishness* (New York: New American Library,
1964), p. 5.

structive or destructive, they determine our values. Thus, if you value good health, you'll avoid activities that are detrimental to health. If you value financial security, you'll conserve your resources instead of being a spend-thrift. If you value a reputation for honesty, you'll be truthful and avoid deceit.

You accumulate your values as you go through life by having experiences you subsequently judge as *good-for-me* or *bad-for-me*. When you have the same experience often enough and reach the same judgment all (or most) of the time, the judgment becomes automatic. This proc-ess makes it possible to quickly answer the question, "Do you like rhubarb pie?" If you couldn't "automate" your value judgments, you would have to stop and think about all the times you've had rhubarb pie and whether you liked it or not on each of those occasions before you could answer yes or no.

Fortunately, you don't have to clutter up your conscious mind with thousands of recollections of hundreds of thousands of experiences. You *integrate* these experi-ences into a pattern of values and value judgments. This pattern is one aspect of personality differences since we don't all value the same things or value them equally.

The things you value—and *dis*value—define you as a person. Do you have certain qualities in which you take pride? Do other people admire you for those qualities? Whatever those qualities may be, they can be traced to values you hold. Do some people dislike you for some qualities in which you take pride? That dislike can be traced to differences between your values and the values of the people who dislike you. Do you sometimes wonder why you "feel" certain things or make certain choices? You wonder because you aren't aware of the values involved in the emotions and choices. Do you have mysteriously contradicting emotions at times? The mystery would be solved if you were aware of the contradictory values that produced the emotions.

What you value, fail to value, or disvalue plays a central role in your life. In your romantic life values govern your choice of partners—their character, appearance, personality, sense of life. They also establish the nature of your relationships—sovereign and equal, dependent, exploitive, of long or short duration—and the level of happiness you will experience. Second only to individual sovereignty, knowledge of the values that control your romantic life is your best assurance of romantic happiness.

Romance-Values

There are three key romance-values that are universal because they reflect fundamental aspects of human psychology: emotional visibility, shared values, and sexual visibility.

Emotional visibility. We desire to be seen and understood by others in the same light as we see and understand ourselves. That is, we desire to have our own self-estimate confirmed by the manner in which others act toward us. If you see yourself as honest, you want the experience of having others behave toward you in a way that is appropriate for dealing with an honest person. If someone treats you as if you are *dis*honest, you don't feel that you've been understood—you feel psychologically *invisible.**

Visibility is important in every relationship. In romantic relationships it is so important that without it the relationship will certainly fail. For example:

Jill said, "I ran into an old boy friend from high school whom I hadn't seen in twelve years. I vaguely remembered how I'd felt about him when I was fifteen, and I was intrigued with the thought of getting to know what he was like now. One evening we were discussing independence and I said, 'I don't feel the need to be taken care of. I'm totally capable of caring for myself; I know what I want and a caveman isn't it.'

"Larry couldn't grasp this. He said, 'Come on, every woman in the world wants the security of having a man around to take care of her. If you're honest with yourself you'll admit it.'

" 'But *I* don't, Larry,' I said. 'I don't need or want a father-image. I got over that years ago.'

"Larry's comment was, 'Okay, but when the right man comes into your life, you'll drop your independence for

* Branden, *The Psychology of Self-Esteem.*

54

a bed and an apron.' Well, we had discussions like that for three months until one day, the final day, he said, 'Quit trying to act like the big sophisticate. Don't forget, I knew you when you were only fifteen, and in spite of all these independent attitudes you say you have, you haven't really changed. You'll come back down to earth and realize that you can't fool yourself or me into believing you really mean these things.'

"Well, that was it. I realized I didn't really care one way or another what he thought. I just wasn't interested in continuing the discussions *or* the relationship."

Lee had a similar experience, but in a relationship of longer standing. It was, as she put it, "a disaster."

"Carl was away for a couple of weeks on business. While he was away, I decided to go boating with another friend of mine who happened to be a man. I called Carl's mother to let her know where I was going so that he wouldn't think I'd died when he got home. When I returned, he was so angry I couldn't believe it.

"He said, 'How could you go away to the shore with that man.' I couldn't understand because he knew that this man was a friend of mine. I said, 'Did it ever occur to you that a man and a woman can do things together without sleeping together?' His answer was 'NO.'

"Now I was really shocked. Where has he been? I thought. It occurred to me that he really had no understanding of the fact that I have a lot of male friends I don't sleep with. I was surprised and disgusted. And insulted. I explained and he didn't believe me. That got me. That did it."

Neither Jill nor Lee (nor you or I, when it happens to us) could continue a relationship in which they were so completely invisible.

Shared values. The second universal romance value is shared values, by which I mean a close correspondence of the value structure of two people. If you share an appreciation of art with your lover—especially the same kind of art, sports, food, literature, politics, and so on— the sharing becomes an emotional bond. The pleasure derived from these shared concretes is palpable; you don't have to think about this kind of sharing, you can *feel* it. The very existence of many shared concretes indicates a deeper sharing: the sharing of underlying values that give rise to the appreciation of the concretes.

It's also possible to share underlying values without sharing particular concretes. For example, you may have a deep appreciation of sculpture and be neutral about music, while your lover's feeling is just the reverse; yet both may make artistic judgments by the same set of aesthetic principles.

Shared values is experienced as one of the highest romance-values because it's a confirmation of our life experience. It means that you and your lover have reached similar conclusions, have learned to value the same things, have perceived the *good-for-me* and *bad-for-me* in much the same way. Because your lover has had a life different from yours, regardless of the amount of similarity, this commonality confirms your own values and conveys to you a sense of having made the "correct" choices and judgments. You may indeed have made all the wrong judgments, but if your lover has made similar wrong judgments, you'll feel a sense of confirmation all the same.

Sexual visibility. The third universal romance-value is sexual self-experience. Everyone has a view, consciously or unconsciously, of their own sexual identity—maleness or femaleness. You need and desire to experience that sexual identity, and you do so primarily in romantic relationships.

Sexual self-experience—or sexual visibility—is not merely the knowledge that we are sexually capable. We don't think of our sexual nature merely in terms of an ability to engage in sexual activity. Our sexual self-image includes the conviction that we are *worthy* of being responded to sexually; that we represent values which are important enough, by our own standards, to make sexual response from others appropriate. For example, a talented and intelligent woman would not experience sexual visibility from a man who responded only to her appearance but not to her mind. It would not be satisfying to her.

Beyond these three universal romantic values, many of the values that influence your romantic choices are the same ones that influence your choices socially. If, for example, you value honesty, you'll probably not knowingly enter a romantic relationship with a dishonest person. Other romance-values are so uniquely personal it is pointless to try to analyze them. When working to identify your romance-values, be warned that it's especially hard to get beyond the obvious to the hidden or obscure. If you seriously and honestly attempt to discover your romantic values, you'll find some that you never knew were there. They may be surprising, or even disconcerting, but nonetheless, they are there and at work when you make romantic choices.

Romance-values and sovereignty. Romance-values may either support sovereignty or subvert it. Pro-sovereignty romance-values are *positive* and anti-sovereignty ones are *negative.* However, in using these terms care must be taken to keep the concepts of *good* and *bad* from creeping in. If a romance-value is *positive,* all that is being said is that it supports sovereignty; no moral judgment has been made about it. Likewise, if a romance-value is *negative,* all that is being said is that it undercuts sovereignty.

I know a man who romantically values aggressive, competitive women. He wants his lover(s) to be competitive with him, both intellectually and physically. I've heard other people criticize that romance-value as "bad" because such a personality is too abrasive for successful romance. Well, those people are entitled to their own opinions and values, but in no way is that romance-value "bad." If the man wants his romantic life to include intellectual and physical competitiveness, he is supporting his sovereignty by having that particular romance-value.

Romance-values that you choose consciously and without outside pressures are *positive* because they reflect your free, unhampered choice. If, for example, you love music and you value the same feeling in your lover, your sovereignty is clearly being served.

Negative romance-values are adopted in response to outside pressures. The most common negative romance-values are culturally inspired. For example, it's the norm in middle-class society for women to marry men who are a few years older, somewhat better educated, and motivated toward financial success. Women who marry men who are younger, less educated, or less ambitious are considered to have "settled" for less than the best.

Now it is entirely possible for a woman to fall in love with a man who shares her general and romantic values and gives her psychological and sexual visibility, but doesn't measure up to these cultural expectations. If this woman denies or represses her romantic response to such a man, or worse still, consciously limits her romantic responses to men who meet these culturally inspired expectations, she will be responding to a *negative* romance-value. She'll have ignored *positive* values and undercut her sovereignty by allowing culture to decide what her romantic responses will be.

Every society has values it seeks to promote. There are cultural romance-values tied to race, religion, earning power, physical types, political ideology, occupation, and so on. By and large, these values are adopted at such an early age they're accepted without question, even when they're in direct conflict with other, clearly recognizable values.

Akin to cultural romance-values is another type that can be called *stereotyped* romance-values. Unlike cultural romance-values, which are imposed from without, you impose stereotyped romance-values on yourself. For example, you may decide that you can respond only to people who have brown eyes or are Scorpios or are at least six feet tall.

Through the process of stereotyping, you classify people and deprive them of their individuality, their uniqueness, their special identity. Stereotyping not only strips others of their individuality in a romantic context, it conflicts with your positive romance-values and undercuts sovereignty. If such casual classifications affect your romantic responses, you fail to allow your real values and needs to guide you in making romantic choices.

HIERARCHY OF VALUES

Of all the things you value, what do you value most? Which values will you choose over which other values? It's obvious that you're able to choose between values most of the time, but how do you do it?

You do it by arranging your values into a hierarchy, a ranking by importance. There are four broad categories of value importance. *High values* are things you consider important to your life, such as a good harvest if you are a farmer. *Low values* are things you consider of marginal importance to your life, such as rain next Tuesday. *Nonvalues* are things you consider irrelevant to your life, such as rain next Tuesday somewhere else. *Disvalues* are things that are harmful to your life, such as rain next Tuesday if you must harvest a field of wheat that day.

Your values, whatever they are, are arranged in a hierarchical order that guides you in making choices. You like chocolate ice cream and dislike coconut cake, so when given a choice between them, you choose the ice cream. Sounds simple, doesn't it?

It is simple—until you get into the tougher choices. For example: Should you take a job you know you'd love in a city you know you'd hate? Or: You're incurably allergic to a pet you love deeply. Should you give up the pet to rid yourself of the discomfort, or put up with the discomfort in order to keep and enjoy the pet?

It's easy to choose between a high value and a low value, nonvalue, or disvalue, but it's often difficult to choose between two values on the same level of importance. Most people are not consciously aware of their hierarchy of values; they do not need to be for most of their values —the less crucial ones. We go through life integrating our value judgments on chocolate ice cream and coconut cake without attaching much importance to the process. Unfortunately, people often take the same cavalier attitude about important values; and when they really need their hierarchy for an important choice, they can't find it. Or worse yet, they don't even know they have one!

Discovering Your Hierarchy of Values

How can you go about discovering your hierarchy of values? There is no perfect way for everyone, but here are some suggestions.

First, don't attempt to deal with every facet of your life all at once. Tackle one aspect at a time, starting with something you've given a lot of thought to in the past—your job, for example.

Second, be aware of the four broad categories of value importance: high values, low values, nonvalues, and disvalues. If you are really serious, make separate lists for each category.

Third, list as many specific values as you can think of in each category. For example, in considering your job, the following values might appear on a high-value list:

1. clear-cut, sole responsibility for assigned duties
2. supervisory responsibility (or no supervisory responsibility)
3. no fixed timetables, prefer to work to a due date (or prefer to work to a detailed timetable)
4. contact with the public (or no public contact)

Disvalues will often be the opposite of high values, and your disvalue category can be extremely valuable in discovering high values. For example, if you know that travel is a disvalue, it will be obvious that not having to travel on a job is a high value. In the same way, low values and nonvalues are often opposites, though not as consistently.

The hard part begins after you have made your first list. In working with people on their hierarchies, I've discovered that most first attempts are singularly lacking in obscure or hidden values. That is, the values listed are more or less common and not always helpful in understanding past actions or current problems.

Larry, for example, showed me his hierarchy and commented that it didn't explain a period in his work life during which he'd become extremely dissatisfied with three successive good jobs, from all of which he had resigned. His present job was, by several standards, not as good as the three he left, but he was very satisfied with it nevertheless.

Eileen began to question Larry about the details of the jobs. She discovered that on the three unsatisfactory ones he had been working under a woman boss, and he was presently working under a male boss. When it was suggested that "women bosses" were a disvalue, Larry angrily denied it; but the following week he acknowledged that, on reflection, he did have a bias against working under a woman's supervision.

* * *

That is what I mean by the obscure or hidden values in your hierarchy. The chances are you have high values, low values, or disvalues that you are not aware of. These unconscious (or subconscious) values may contradict some of your conscious values, or they may not be particularly attractive to you for some reason. (They may even be the result of some irrational bias or prejudice that you carry around in your subconscious.) If you're going to understand your hierarchy of values, you'll need to become conscious of all your values. If you don't, the unknown ones will continue to influence your behavior, and you'll be at a loss to understand it.

One of the best ways of discovering unknown values or disvalues is the way it happened in Larry's case. When you've worked on your hierarchy in one or all aspects of your life, look back at decisions you've made in the past and see if they can be explained by the values on your hierarchy. If not, you've either missed something or your values have changed since then.

Getting your hierarchy out in the open is the best way of looking into the future to see if you are really headed in the direction you think you want. If Larry works in a field where women bosses are to be expected, and if he wants to get to the top of that field, his hierarchy is standing in the way *if* his bias is stronger than his desire to succeed. Something's got to give!

Discovering your romantic hierarchy may be especially tricky at first. Many people believe that if they analyze their romantic emotions they'll lose the spontaneity and joy of loving. To the contrary, all they'll lose is the handicap of living their romantic lives by whim and guess-work.

To begin the task, keep in mind the four levels of value importance: high values, low values, nonvalues, and dis-values. Don't disregard nonvalues since that category will help you identify things you consider irrelevant. Many of these irrelevancies may be the values of The Myth, such as "having children" or "steady income."

Next, devise categories of romantic-values by subject matter, perhaps as follows:

Character traits: values, goals, viewpoints
Personality traits: temperament, sense of humor, style
Appearance: physique, mode of dress
Sexual attitudes: appetites, fantasies, expressiveness
Intellectual/recreational interests: education, hob-bies, causes
Life-style: vocation, home/work/fun orientation, stability

For each category you use, list your values by level of importance. The following is from a woman's romantic hierarchy:

Sexual attitudes. My values to be matched in a man

High values: Experimental, curious, energetic and vocal
Enjoy nudity
Especially enjoy sex in the morn-ing

Sex in places other than bed

Low values: (Nothing. Sex issues are either plus, negative, or neutral for me but *never* lukewarm.)

Nonvalues: Simultaneous orgasm—any sequence is terrific!

Disvalues: Sex by schedule

Complete darkness for sex

Body shyness

Disliking one-sided sex (I like to make love even when I don't want to be made love to, and vice versa.)

This particular hierarchy doesn't appear to have any obscure or hidden romantic-values, but here are some examples of idiosyncratic romantic-values I've come across in myself and others:

1. On physical attributes I found these values. Among women: men with "hairy muscular arms with prominent veins," "firm, small ass," "fair (light) body hair," "big feet." Among men: women with "muscular dancer's legs," "kinky black hair," "slight double-chin."

2. On emotional and personality traits. Among women: men "with a need for closeness with nature," "who are a little dominating without being overbearing," "who are slightly awesome." Among men: women who "talk like a man," "are too independent to ever consider marriage," "are mechanically inclined."

3. On sexual attitudes. Among women: men who "are earthy, even vulgar in bed," "often submissive in mak-

ing love." Among men: women who "are assertive and often take the initiative in sex," "have a lot of fantasies and want to act them out."

If you will get your romantic hierarchy out in the open, you'll begin to understand many of the romantic choices you've made in the past and be better prepared for the future. Knowing your hierarchies, both general and romantic, is the first step in rearranging your values and that is the first step in restructuring your emotional responses to serve your sovereignty.

CHANGING YOUR EMOTIONAL PATTERNS

Because emotions come from value judgments which in turn depend on values, changes in emotional patterns require the adoption and integration ("automation") of (1) new values, (2) reappraisal of inappropriate old values into disvalues, and (3) realignment of hierarchies.

Adopting new values begins with *thinking*. If equality in a romantic relationship has never been a value to you, the first step is to think about the issue. Why is equality important? What emotional price do you pay for unequal relationships? How have unequal relationships diminished your potential for happiness? In what ways would equality benefit your present relationships? What values do you now hold that prevent equality in your relationships?

Think about it. Think about sovereignty, autonomy, and slavery; authoritarianism and ownership trips; poachers, predators, insecurity, and emotional blackmail. Think about differences and whether you use them for growth.

If your thinking leads you to the conclusion that *equality* is a *value,* say it. Say it to your lover, say it to your friends, say it to anyone who shows the slightest interest in discussing the subject. Saying it and saying it often is the start of integrating it, of building up the habit of *valuing* it.

Along with saying it, remember the thinking that led to saying it. Remember the thinking when you do or say something that contradicts your new value, *equality*. That will happen, of course, and happen frequently at first. When it does, think and say that the contradiction comes from an old value that's now a disvalue and identify that disvalue as accurately as you can. (That may require more thinking.) Now you have a new *value* and a growing list of *disvalues* to think about and talk about. Do it often; it builds up the habit of valuing and disvaluing.

And then there's action. Act on the basis of your new value, and don't act on your new disvalue. When a contradictory emotion pops up (based on an old value turned disvalue), don't act on it; act as if the desired emotion occurred instead. If you discover that a difference between you and your lover is eating away at your relationship, firmly decide whether that difference is terminal. If not, instead of letting it fester, turn it into a means of growth. Adopt it, try it, understand it. Find out if the difference represents a better way, or a new and enjoyable way, or just a different but equally valid way. If you can't adopt it as another alternative for your-self, accept it as your lover's way and consider it irrele-vant to your relationship. (If you can't after all that, it's probably terminal!)

This process that begins with thinking and continues through action will rearrange your hierarchies. New values will arrange themselves, old values turned dis-values will eventually be displaced. Just thinking about and working with your values will clarify which values are higher than others. When that's clear, choosing a higher value over a lower value becomes easier and more satisfying. You'll begin to lose the frustration of giving up certain things because you'll know you're giving them up for other things that are more important to you.

Yes, you can change your values. If you do, your con-scious value judgments will change, and eventually your automatic value judgments—your emotional responses—will also change. Most people have experienced changes in emotional responses over a period of time, and a little introspection will usually uncover the changes in values that are responsible.

The following is an example of a change in values. The subject of the interview, Ann, is a professional woman, about thirty years old.

JK: Did you ever fall victim to the pressure that turns a casual relationship into a tight, exclusive one when that really wasn't what you wanted the relationship to be?

ANN: Absolutely. But it's easier now, what with all the current literature on feminism, for women to accept the idea that they can have a relationship with more than one person at a time. Ten years ago that idea never occurred to me. I didn't have any basis for challenging the old idea. I mean, one just didn't. I was just able to be comfortable, not really too comfortable, with the idea that I was going to have sexual relationships before marriage. The idea that I would have more than one such relationship at a time because there was no one particular person I wanted to devote all my time to . . . well, I didn't have the framework for that. Had it been proposed to me I would have been kind of mixed up, thinking of myself as a "loose woman" or something like that.

The first few times after my divorce I made a lot of trouble for myself. I was seeing one nice young man who wasn't prepared for an exclusive relationship and I really wasn't either, but somehow it just didn't seem right to me that he had another woman. The next time I got involved, he was pretty good and I wanted to have a continuing but nonexclusive relationship with him, but he wasn't thinking that way. He didn't have any framework for a "nice girl" to have other men and so I just fell into a monogamous thing for quite a while. I finally reordered it, though, and said, "This just isn't what I want. I don't see it as being forever and ever. It's good and if you want to see

me, fine, but I want to see other people." But that
was very hard. It took me a while to get free.

JK: Hard on you to get out of the old way of thinking?
ANN: Yes, emotionally . . . very hard. It was very
painful to get out of that monogamous thing even
though I wanted out. I had to find the feeling that,
well, there are all kinds of men out there and although we had this good thing going and I liked
it, it wasn't enough for me. I wanted to have some
other kinds of things with other kinds of men.
When I finally did, it was really terrific!

Ann started out with a value—monogamy—supplied by
her cultural context; after realizing that this value wasn't
what she really wanted, she replaced it with another.
Her statement, "When I finally did, it was really terrific!" makes it clear that there's been a change from her
old emotional response of "loose woman."

You too can change your emotional responses by changing your values and value judgments. Here's how:

1. Think about your values consciously instead of merely
   absorbing them from the outside. Use your own standards to judge yourself, your job, your life-style, your
   lover, and other people. Be clear about what you expect from yourself and others, and refuse to settle for
   less. By consciously *applying* your values to real-life
   situations, you'll "automate" them.
2. Resolve your value conflicts as you discover them.

Old habits won't be banished outright; they can only be replaced by new and stronger habits. If you are consciously aware of the values you now hold, conflicts with old values won't pass unnoticed. If, for example, you consciously value your sovereignty, you'll be aware of abdicating it if that occurs. Think it through. Why are you abdicating? What value do you think you are protecting by your abdication? Is that value a higher one than your sovereignty? To resolve a value conflict, always assert the higher of the values involved.

3. Make sure your conscious value judgments and actions are consistent with your consciously held values. If, for instance, you value independence and someone tries to saddle you with their dependence, recognize that for what it is and act accordingly. If you accept their dependence you are creating a value conflict. If you reject it you are "automating" your own value.

4. Think through each emotional response that you suspect may originate in old, discarded values. Suppose that in the past you've been prone to jealousy and you experience a flash of anger or suspicion when your lover informs you that they want to be alone for a week. Don't banish that emotional response from your mind and let it go at that. The fact that you experienced it means that an old or heretofore unconscious value is at work causing the response. Think about it. Try to discover why you felt as you did. Is it the old problem again? Then go through your reasons, again, for giving up those old jealousy-producing values. Is it a new problem? Then work to dis-

cover it, and when you succeed, decide how you are going to deal with it.

If this sounds like a lot of effort, remember the reward for success makes it all worthwhile. That reward is confidence in your emotional responses, the confidence that comes from knowing that your emotions can be "trusted" to promote your happiness rather than interfere with it.

We are constantly faced with situations that must be judged on scanty and incomplete information. If we know that our emotional responses are consistent and dependable reflections of our *chosen* values, we can rely on them as a guide to action.

love

Ask a random sample of people to tell you what *romantic love* is, and the result will resemble the allegory of the three blind men trying to describe an elephant: none of the descriptions will be alike. Part of the problem is the word *romantic*. It's become associated with King Arthur, Camelot, Sir Lancelot, and the tradition of "courtly" emotional game playing.

Well, we're no longer jousting in tournaments or traveling two thousand miles on horseback to fight wars with swords and lances. But many people are still dealing with romantic love as if it's either a game or an unrealizable ideal. If love is a game there'll be winners and losers, and no possibility of equal relationships. As for being an unrealizable ideal, all myths are beyond realization: we need to set aside The Myth so we can see and live with the reality.

The Myth is culture's view of romantic love. It is two lives becoming one; dedicating your life to the happiness of your mate; desiring your mate above all others, till death do you part.

However, some critics think The Myth is culturally approved mass neurosis. Considering the gap between reality and The Myth, mass neurosis is a reasonable judgment.

What then is *love?* Just as we learn to identify jealousy by the standard of behavior, we learn to identify love by the same standard. We're taught that certain kinds of behavior are the result or evidence of feeling love. By the time we are in our mid-teens we've also learned (from literature, movies and other cultural sources) that romantic love entails certain consequences. (The Myth is behavioral as well as emotional; it tells us what to do as well as what to feel.) By the same process described earlier relative to jealousy we come to associate the *emotion* love—romantic and otherwise—with certain kinds of behavior. As a result little or no attention is paid to the nature and meaning of the emotion itself.

Trying to define an emotion is as pointless as trying to describe the taste of an orange without referring to the tastes of other objects. (Try it!) However, a precise definition of the emotion you feel when you "love" isn't important (even if it's possible, which I doubt) because love, when you experience it, is *self-evident*. You don't

need a definition when you love someone; you know what
it is. What's more, you also know the *kind* of love you're
feeling.

Consider the love you feel for your child, your parents,
and your friends. These experiences are self-evident, as
are the distinctions between them. They're distinctively
different because the values that give rise to the emotions
are different. You value your children because they are
(probably) the objectification of the love you feel (or
felt) for the other parent; because they are at once separate beings and extensions of your own being; because
in nurturing and experiencing the child you have shared
many deep emotions and given and received visibility.
You value your parents because of the care and love
they've given you, among many other possible reasons.
You love your friends because of the values they hold,
the things you share, and the visibility you receive from
them.

The *experience* of these three "kinds" of love may well
be almost identical, but you won't confuse one with the
others because different values and contexts are involved.
These differences lead you to express, or act on, your
emotions in different ways for each kind of love-object.

Romantic love is equally self-evident and distinct. Many
of the romance-values on your hierarchy can never apply
to children, parents, and friends. The experience of visibility and the desire to share will be more intense in
romantic love than in other kinds of love. Then, there's
the difference that is absolutely distinctive: the need for
a fullness of expression that can only be achieved

through sexual intimacy. The level of intimacy will be higher in every respect, and it isn't likely that this breadth and intensity of feeling and expression will occur toward nonromantic (platonic) love-objects.

Recognizing the self-evidency of romantic love may not appear to be connected with sovereignty, but it is. Society has set standards for "love" that have little or nothing to do with what we feel; and if we accept them, our sovereignty is undercut. The Myth says love, "true love" (whatever *that* is), is exclusive, forever, selfless, duty-laden, and totally satisfying. If you think you're in love but don't feel all the things The Myth says you must, presumably it's not "true love." It must then be false love.

But experience teaches otherwise. You've felt romantic love without feeling that the relationship was forever or totally satisfying. You've felt love without feeling exclusive or selfless or obligated to duties. And you've felt love even while recognizing that your lover wasn't everything you needed in your romantic life. But, with all that, if it felt like love to you, it was love. And if you acknowledged it as such, you were living by your own standards, not The Myth's.

Romantic love isn't the single, narrowly defined condition The Myth insists upon. It is as varied as any other category of human relationships. It exists with and without commitment, with and without permanence, with many or few common values, and with or without any resemblance between your experience of love and mine.

Because not everyone experiences love the same way, not everyone chooses the same kind of love-object. Homosexual and bisexual romantic love are as valid as heterosexual love. They're all love if they are so experienced. *Mandatory heterosexuality* is as much a part of The Myth as, say, *commitment*. Labeling homosexuality and bisexuality as neurotic ignores the extensive amount of neurosis found in society's heterosexuality. It's not the choice of love-object that identifies neurotic sex; it's the neurosis of the individuals.

This comment on choice of love-object wouldn't be complete without looking at another part of society's Myth: the incest taboo. Anthropologists and geneticists agree that the incest taboo has nothing to do with preventing genetic destruction of the species. To the contrary, over long periods of time incest would breed *out* harmful and deadly recessive genetic traits. That these traits still exist is the result of the taboo, not the validation of it.

The narrow choice of romantic love-objects tolerated by The Myth isn't consistent with actual human capacities for feeling romantic love. You may not be at all interested in homosexuality or marrying your first cousin, but to see The Myth in true perspective you should be aware of the artificiality of its imposed limitations.

If you're in love with someone, you know it. If you're in love with two people, you know that as well; but you may not know why. The differences between two or more concurrent experiences of romantic love aren't necessarily self-evident.

If you've ever been content in a romantic relationship for more or less extended periods of time and then began to have romantic feelings for someone new, as likely as not these new emotions made you feel disloyal, unfaithful, and guilty. If you didn't understand why you were in love with the first person, there was little chance of understanding why you'd fall in love with the second. Obviously, there was some "space" in your romantic life which the new person could occupy; but unless you understand your own emotions, how could you retain perspective?

Why the new feelings of love? Have you stopped loving your first partner? Are you bored and fickle, or are there values and needs being met in the second relationship that weren't met in the first? Does the second relationship satisfy the same values and needs as the first?

DIFFERENTIATING ROMANTIC RESPONSES

Being aware of your romantic hierarchy assists you in differentiating romantic responses on the basis of the values and needs being met in a given relationship. Therefore, satisfaction of values and needs is a *scale of measurement.*

If you knew your romantic hierarchy in detail, including the relative importance of every value, you'd also know the strengths, weaknesses, and long-range potential of each relationship. Unfortunately, that isn't likely to be the case, and conclusions drawn from using this scale of measurement may turn out to be at odds with your feelings. After identifying, as clearly as possible, the values and needs underlying a certain romantic relationship, you may decide that the relationship isn't based upon what you think are high values. If the emotion felt is, nevertheless, experienced as *strong,* the contradiction between what you *think* you should be feeling and what you know you're *actually feeling* can be the cause of emotional distress and self-doubt.

In such circumstances you are faced with choosing between your intellectual analysis of the situation—your understanding of the needs and values being met—and the self-evident strength of the emotions you feel. If you have confidence in your emotions, you're likely to abandon the intellectual analysis when faced with that choice.

Thus, strength of response is another scale of measurement; but it, too, can be inadequate for successful differentiation. You may be responding to a transient value or need. *Any* value can be transient. For example, people who find themselves suddenly alone after a divorce or some other involuntary and permanent ending of a happy life situation may elevate companionship (or even more to the point, availability) to a high place on their hierarchy. When a transient value occupies a high place on your hierarchy, for however short a time, it can become the basis for an initially strong romantic response that will fade as the importance of the transient value fades.

Another failing of strength as a scale of measurement refers to *rarely met* values and needs which may or may

80

not be high on your hierarchy. This situation can evoke extremely strong romantic responses because of the rarity with which the value or need is satisfied. Imagine meeting a potential lover who satisfies and reflects a value of great importance, one that you've never before experienced in another person. For example, you might value art highly and meet a talented painter. The importance of the value could provoke an extremely strong response, even if it was the only major value satisfied by that person.

This kind of exceptional experience can cause strong romantic response simply because it is exceptional. If, in such a circumstance, you think, "I've never felt this way before," it's probably true. You haven't felt *exactly* this way because the value involved hasn't been satisfied before; the emotional experience *is* different, if not unique.

When Allan met Marni he was attracted to her style and appearance, but the relationship limped along for several months without developing any kind of deep bond. The relationship was about to expire when they unexpectedly found themselves in a sexually charged situation that led to making love.

For years Allan had been developing a fantasy about the "perfect" sexual relationship, and Marni turned out to be it. It was, Allan said, double-dynamite; but after six months they knew that sex was the only major thing they had in common and that they were in direct conflict on just about everything else.

The relationship had always been stormy, except in bed, but it began to turn vicious. As the frequency of the brawls increased, sex decreased; finally, the relationship blew apart in a fight that could be heard for miles and required armed intervention by the police.

Looking back, Allan admits, "I never felt that way about a woman before." He's sure that what he felt was love, but that one value—sex—as important as it was, wasn't enough. Of course, you can't absolutely rule out the possibility of a successful long-term relationship built on only one value. There *are* lovers who have only one important value in common, but most people aren't so singleminded.

Both strength of response and reference to your values may not be adequate scales of measurement for differentiating romantic responses. Ideally, you'll try to use both; and if you're really in touch with yourself, perhaps they'll be sufficient. If not, it would be helpful to have other tools available.

AN ALTERNATIVE—AND OFFBEAT— SCALE OF MEASUREMENT

In looking for other means of measuring romantic responses, we're limited to two basic approaches—intellect and feelings. With all due respect to intellect, we're dealing with emotions, and a scale of measurement that worked on an emotional level would be especially useful.

When you have a romantic response to someone, that *person* becomes something you value. If you achieve a romantic relationship with that person, the relationship produces, or contributes to, a state of happiness for you. This happy state itself is self-evident, and the cause-and-effect relationship between your lover and the happy state is also self-evident.

Now, just as you know that both your lover and the relationship are high values, you know from experience that when you lose important values, you experience a *sense* of loss. You also know from experience that the magnitude of the loss varies with the importance of the lost value. If you are unfortunate enough to lose a value that is crucial to your present happiness, the resulting sense of loss is deep, profound, *tragic*. If the lost value is *not* crucial to your present happiness, the sense of loss will not be as great; and if the lost value is irrelevant to your happiness, the sense of loss will be minimal. (If any value, no matter how small, is lost, some sense of loss will be felt.)

When you want to measure the emotional importance of a romantic relationship, ask yourself, "If I were deprived of this relationship, if it were no longer possible to share my life with my lover, how great a sense of loss would I experience?" This question shifts your attention from both strength of response and values satisfied. If you are sufficiently in touch with yourself, you can focus your feelings on the *impact* of the imagined loss of the relationship. If, then, you realize that being deprived of the relationship would produce only regret, or moderate sadness, or even more neutral emotions, you can be reasonably sure that the relationship is of only *moderate* emotional importance to you. (Even so, you may *still* be feeling a strong response and that tells you the response is both strong *and* only moderately important to your present emotional happiness.) On the other hand, if you realize that you'd experience a deep and profound sense of loss, you'd then know how emotionally *important* that relationship is.

Sarah was involved with two men, Tom and Horst. Though not sexually involved with both, the fact of having two emotionally important relationships bothered her. She had known Tom for over two years. They met in a sketching class and enjoyed sharing music, galleries, and sketching around the city and Central Park. Sarah felt very "with" Tom, very close to him.

Horst was physical. Sarah had known him not quite a year, and although they weren't living together, she loved him and sex with him was terrific.

What was bothering her was a growing sexual desire for Tom. When I said I wasn't surprised and that it sounded quite appropriate, she said, "Well, it sure doesn't seem appropriate to me. My sex life has never been better and I don't know if I can handle two lovers. I just don't see how I can feel that way about Tom with Horst around."

I asked her how she'd feel if her relationship with Tom came to an end, and she said, "Terrible. That would be just awful. I get so much out of being with him." Then I

other than what you have agreed to do. The concept of voluntarism can only apply to a situation in which you have the explicit freedom to choose between alternatives.

By agreeing in advance to confine your romantic emotional responses to your lover—or, failing that, agreeing not to act upon such responses you may have—you have abdicated your sovereignty. Romantic emotional responses are based on values, and a formal agreement to confine those responses to one person implies an obligation to repress any others. You may, over a period of time—even a long time—actually respond romantically to only one person. But realistically, there's no way short of repression for you to agree to do so in advance.

This unrealistic agreement has always needed a justification. In the past, the agreement bound women more than men, and there wasn't much finesse used in justifying it. Men had more power than women; they established the rules. Therefore, women were required to be physically and emotionally monogamous. As women freed themselves from explicit chattelization, the arguments supporting monogamy became more intellectual. Now monogamy rests upon religious morality supported by certain assertions about the psychological nature of humankind.

THREE ARGUMENTS FOR
COERCIVE ROMANTIC MONOPOLIES

The Myth promotes romantic exclusivity through three assertions:

1. the presumed indivisibility of "authentic" romantic love
2. the presumed need for commitment and continuity
3. the presumed increase in sharing and intimacy resulting from exclusivity

The 100 Percent Rule

The first of these assertions, that authentic romantic love is indivisible, I call the *100 Percent Rule*. This rule maintains that authentic (or "true") love is indivisible; it can't be felt for more than one person at a time. To this must be added two interesting corollaries:

1. Emotional (read "sexual") responses to more than one person at a time are, per se, something other than "true love," that is, "Don Juan-ism," "nymphomania," "animal lust," etc.
2. Anyone who claims to love more than one person at a time romantically is really professing their inability to "love" at all; such a claim is prima facie evidence of an emotional deficiency.

The above is, of course, nonsense. Do you love each of your friends less than if you had only one friend? Do you expect that having two children will result in loving each child only half as much as would be the case if you had only one child? Is there any category of love, other than romantic love, in which your capacity to love is presumed to be reduced because you have more than one love-object?

Suppose, for a moment, that you have one hundred values on your romantic hierarchy, and you're in love with someone who reflects seventy-five of them. (For simplicity's sake, ignore how these seventy-five are ranked in importance.) Later on, you meet and eventually begin to love someone who also reflects seventy-five of your values, and of those seventy-five, sixty are also reflected by your first lover and fifteen are not.

Now you have ninety of your values reflected in your romantic life, and each lover reflects fifteen values that the other doesn't. *All other things being the same,* you'll probably love each person equally.

However, the 100 Percent Rule asserts that this can't be so—that what you are feeling is *not* authentic or "true" love. But, love is the result of a response to values and its existence is self-evident. No one can tell you that what you feel isn't love when you know it is!

The 100 Percent Rule undercuts sovereignty by creating a qualification by which a lover can, for authoritarian reasons, presume to judge the authenticity of your romantic responses. That is to say, if you have more than one romantic relationship, by appealing to the 100 Percent Rule, a lover can accuse you of not feeling "true love," or worse, not being able to love at all. If you believe the accusation and decide to suppress some of your romantic responses, you are abdicating your sovereignty.

Remember, when you have romantic responses toward someone, you have them for specific reasons—because that person reflects and satisfies values and needs on your romantic hierarchy. That is the basis of the authenticity of your response. Whether or not you have romantic responses for anyone else is irrelevant. If you have them, you have them. That's the reality of your emotional life at that time. Barring the influence of the 100 Percent Rule, you'll simply recognize that you love one person for *these* reasons and the other person for *those* reasons. You'll know that the authenticity of both responses is based on the interaction of each lover with your values, not whether you have one lover or more. For this reason you'll experience all romantic responses as equally authentic. It follows, therefore, that if you have authentic romantic emotions for more than one person, sexual expressions of those emotions are equally authentic and appropriate. That is, they're not the result of "Don Juan-ism," "nymphomania," "animal lust," or any of the other unflattering terms used to discourage sexual nonexclusivity.

Keep in mind the distinctions between romantic love and other kinds of love. Romantic love entails:

1. intense desire for sharing
2. heightened sexual visibility
3. desire for and value of sexual intimacy

If you're experiencing all three, you can't arbitrarily suppress the desire for sexual intimacy without denying your own values, that is, abdicating your sovereignty.

Lasting Commitment

The second argument for exclusivity is the presumed need for commitment and continuity. This argument maintains that there's a human need for assurance that our romantic relationships involve a sense of commitment and the prospect of longevity.

To what can you ask your lover to make a commitment? To you? To the relationship itself? What would be the terms of such commitments? Clearly, only two kinds of commitment are possible: sovereign and anti-sovereign.

The anti-sovereign commitment says, in effect: "I commit myself to you regardless of how you (or the relationship) change. I promise to love no other and to remain exclusively yours both emotionally and physically." This, of course, is the conventional commitment of marriage. It may be argued that present-day marriage is less restrictive, but that is a matter of degree only.

On the other hand, a commitment consistent with the declarer's sovereignty would have to go something like this: "I pledge that as long, and only as long, as I feel love for you I will express it." But, such a declaration isn't a commitment to another person or to a relationship. It is a commitment to your own sovereignty.

If you think that a compromise between exclusive commitment and sovereignty is possible, be forewarned that any attempt to describe it will collapse in illogic. The following is one such attempt.

GEORGE: I know marriages and other romantic relationships don't necessarily last forever. Many of them shouldn't, anyway. But while it lasts, I think a commitment *is* important, and exclusivity is the best evidence of that commitment.

JK: All right, you want the commitment, but you know it may not be forever. For how long, then, should you make the commitment?

GEORGE: For as long as the relationship lasts.

JK: Do you mean that the relationship should be formally ended before exclusivity is breached?

GEORGE: Yes.

JK: I see. Then if you and your lover make a commitment today, and a year later your lover wants to end the exclusivity and so announces, you'd feel fairly treated?

GEORGE: Well, I might not be happy about it, but I'd feel I'd been treated fairly, yes.

JK: All right, then, what if it happened in six months?

GEORGE: I'd feel the same.

JK: What about six weeks or six days?

GEORGE: Wait a minute. I'd wonder why my lover made the commitment in the first place, if it lasted only six weeks or six days.

JK: But couldn't the commitment be made in good faith and still only hold up for six weeks or even six days? Isn't that possible?

GEORGE: Yes, it's possible I guess.

JK: Okay, then, would you still feel fairly treated?

GEORGE: I guess so.

JK: All right, now you tell me the difference be-

tween what we've just discussed and the following: I pledge that as long, and only as long,
as I have romantic feelings *only* for you, I'll
not have or express romantic feelings for anyone else.

GEORGE: But that's circular! All you've said is: As long
as I feel for one person, I'll only feel for one
person!

JK: That's right. And your formulation was just as
circular. All you said was: As long as the exclusive relationship lasts, it will be exclusive.
You haven't obtained, in any real sense, a *commitment*. All you have is a recognition that,
since the relationship is defined as exclusive in
the first place, the relationship will last as long
as exclusivity is possible, even if that period
of time is only six days. I fail to see that any
agreement that can be set aside unilaterally at
any time qualifies as a commitment. What is
being committed?

GEORGE: Not much, I guess.

JK: That's right. The only alternative is an agreement that *can't* be set aside unilaterally and
that is clearly a violation of sovereignty. We
are back to the original two alternatives.

The choice is clear enough. You can make a commitment to your own sovereignty, or you can make one that
requires you to abdicate your sovereignty.

The argument for a human *need* for commitment and continuity isn't based on reality. It is true, of course, that some, even many, individuals want the assurance that such a commitment would bring; but that is not to say that *all* people require such assurance. What all people *do* require is the control over their lives that results from unbreached sovereignty.

More to Share, Less Shared

The third argument for exclusivity is the presumed increase in sharing and intimacy that results from exclusivity. The full argument is: Nonexclusivity results in areas of experience that can't be shared with all your lovers because those experiences involve emotional "rivals." Further, inability to share in that respect will eventually erode the ability to share in other respects.

I have no doubt that the real-life model for this argument is the typical husband/wife unit in which one or the other has another lover. Since this model includes the exclusivity clause to begin with, sharing probably won't occur because to share the extramarital experience constitutes a "breach of contract" and an admission of wrongdoing.

However, this model doesn't prove that sharing *must* be reduced by nonexclusivity. It merely suggests that if exclusivity is the rule, the lover who breaks that rule won't be eager to admit it.

The real question is: Is there anything in the nature of nonexclusivity that can be shown to reduce sharing and intimacy between lovers? The answer will be found in the consideration of two further questions:

1. Is there an *actual reduction* of sharing if your lover fails to share "outside" experiences with you?
2. Why wouldn't you want to share your lover's outside experiences?

Is there, then, an actual reduction in sharing? First, recognize that *sovereign* lovers will share to a degree acceptable to each. Sharing may or may not be total, and if it is less than total, the amount will be based upon their own inclinations and choices. A close, intimate relationship does not require a slavish adherence to some arbitrary standard such as "I'll tell you every thought and experience I have and you'll do the same."

In any event, lovers will share to the degree they find acceptable. If either lover has another emotional relationship and doesn't share it, there is no reduction in what the two lovers do share; there is only an absence of an increase. The lack of an increase in sharing isn't the same as a reduction.

The more important question is: Why wouldn't you want to share in your lover's other emotional experiences? I can think of only two reasons why: You are the victim of the poacher/predator mentality (jealousy), or you are afraid that comparisons will be made to your disadvantage.

Since I've already discussed the poacher/predator idea, I'll not repeat it here; but comparisons are another matter. Being fearful of comparisons (with so-called romantic rivals) ignores the basic fundamentals of romantic emotions. Why does your lover love you? Because of the unique person you are. Remember this crucially important truth: You are loved only because of what you are, *not in spite of what you aren't*.

It would be absurd to think that your lover's attitude toward you is summed up as: "Well, he isn't this, isn't that, isn't the other thing, but I love him *despite those failings*." On the contrary, it is your qualities that attract and hold love; the values you hold, the kind of person you are. That being the case, you have nothing to fear from comparisons with others as long as you hold to your individuality.

You are always going to be subjected to comparisons, the primary result of which will be the recognition that you are different from the person with whom you are being compared. In most cases, those differences are the reasons why you are loved in the first place. If, however, your lover finds that you fill a certain need less completely than someone else, that is a fact of life you have to recognize. Declining to share your lover's relationship with that person won't change that fact one bit. Neither will insistence on exclusivity because, although you may avoid the comparison with someone else, you'll never be able to avoid having your lover be aware that you don't fill that certain need adequately.

Comparisons are your ally, not your foe, if you maintain your individuality and sovereignty.

EFFECTS OF COERCIVE ROMANTIC MONOPOLIES

It's true, of course, that until one of the partners in a coercive romantic monopoly actually faces the problem of having a romantic response to someone else, the coercive nature of the monopoly isn't likely to cause any overt problems. However, even a cursory glance at present divorce rates, psychological studies of married people, and the incidence of postmarital "affairs" makes it plain that a very large percentage of people in these coercive monopolies *do* face the problem. When the coercive nature of the monopoly is invoked, the partner who calls upon it is attempting to control their lover's emotional responses. And if the attempt is successful, it has a negative effect on both partners.

The effect on the partner who is on the ownership trip is a loss (or reduction) of the feeling of *efficacy* that is the result of a successful romantic relationship. In the early days of a romance, one of the most exhilarating experiences you have is a feeling of emotional strength. That feeling is the result of knowing that the person you are responding to is responding to you, is choosing you over other available choices. The effect of being valued romantically by someone you value romantically is a feeling of emotional efficacy or strength.

But that feeling occurs only when your lover has—and is free to exercise—the power to accept or reject you. If your lover's freedom of choice has been crippled by succumbing to your ownership trip, you'll be aware (if only dimly) that you are no longer evoking a romantic response based on values, but instead, a response based on psychological dependence. No feelings of efficacy or strength are to be gained from such a realization.

For the partner who is the victim of the ownership trip, a coercive monopoly produces a feeling of loss of control. Feeling in control of your life is crucial to psychological well-being, but how can you experience that feeling if you allow your lover to define the nature and extent of your emotions? *Your* sovereignty and individuality is expressed by *your* values and the choices *you* make. If you abandon your values and hand to your lover your power of choice (including the choice to freely express *all* your emotions), you will become, psychologically, a chattel. You will be *owned*.

Society has a vested interest in perpetuating coercive romantic monopolies because, without them, The Myth would collapse, as would society's control of voluntary sexual behavior. Sovereignty isn't a value to authoritarian society, it's a target. Because the effects of coercive romantic monopolies are anti-sovereignty, society will continue to reserve its full approval for that life-style.

Remember, a romantic monopoly is coercive if:

1. The relationship is not based on psychological laissez faire.
2. The free exercise of sovereignty by either partner constitutes a "breach of contract."
3. Either partner threatens to dissolve the relationship if the other maintains and exercises sovereignty.

NATURAL ROMANTIC MONOPOLY

Romantic exclusivity and sovereignty are not irreconcilable. In the obsessive stage of a romance, lovers usually feel exclusive with little or no emotional energy or sexual desire for anyone but each other. The Myth promises that it will never end; experience tells you it probably will. The Myth makes no provision for the ending of obsessive exclusivity other than *serial monogamy,* but that is cheating on The Myth's principle.

A *natural romantic monopoly* is an exclusive relationship based entirely on voluntarism. That is, the exclusivity exists because one or both of the lovers *feels* exclusive, not because there's been an *agreement to be* exclusive.

One or both lovers. A natural romantic monopoly doesn't necessarily involve *mutual* exclusivity. Because the relationship is voluntary in every respect, it's possible for the exclusiveness to be unilateral.

To repeat, psychological laissez faire is the practice of noninterference in the emotional freedom of others. If one or both lovers in a relationship feel exclusive, that is a fact, a self-evident emotional condition. The natural romantic monopoly recognizes that fact, whether that condition is mutual or not.

The difference between a natural monopoly and the coercive kind is the lack of "contract" or expectation that the exclusivity will continue. *In a natural romantic*

101

monopoly, exclusivity is not a necessary characteristic of the relationship. If exclusivity ends, the *only* change in the relationship will be that the relationship has become nonexclusive. The passing of exclusivity will not be seen as a deterioration of the relationship.

Why is that the *only* change? Why don't either or both partners feel that "something" in the relationship has been lost? Because of the principle of psychological laissez faire. A natural romantic monopoly can't exist except on that principle. Neither lover feels that "something" (that is, *a value*) has been lost because:

1. Exclusivity is not a necessary aspect of the relationship.
2. They adhere to the principle of noninterference in their lover's emotional freedom, and the exercise of emotional sovereignty is a *higher* value than exclusivity.
3. Since they are dedicated to their own sovereignty above all, equality requires similar dedication to the other's sovereignty.

A sovereign person may value exclusivity, but only to the extent that it presupposes a perfect relationship in which *all* values or needs are met to the *fullest* extent. But note that exclusivity is not a prime value, it's a *consequence.* The sovereign person, responding to their own values, won't value a lover's feelings of exclusivity more than they value *the lover.* Therefore, if the lover's feelings of exclusivity end, what has been lost is minimal compared to the value of the lover.

In short, a sovereign person values what a lover is, the kind of person a lover is, not whether that lover feels exclusive.

A *natural romantic monopoly is an equal relationship,* an *exclusive* equal relationship. Equal relationships are devoid of authoritarianism. Equals don't expect more from each other than each is willing to give voluntarily. This voluntarism permits the partners to withstand stresses and strains that destroy unequal relationships.

For example, all human relationships exhibit periodicity. Friendships and nonromantic love relationships with children, parents, and siblings all undergo variations in intensity. Only the romantic love relationship, according to The Myth, isn't supposed to exhibit this trait; and most conventional coercive monopolies aren't prepared to handle it when it occurs. Equal lovers are prepared; they understand (because of their own experience) that emotional energy undergoes changes of focus or intensity for many reasons. The focus of emotional energy may change from romance to work, from there to study and on to introspection; it may retreat from intensity to passivity in order to regain strength; it may change from one love-object to another and return again, undiminished.

Natural romantic monopolies can accommodate such changes even when the result moves the relationship from exclusive to nonexclusive and back again. Since exclusivity is recognized as an emotional condition rather than an obligation, loss of feelings of exclusivity isn't the traumatizing event it would be for nonequal lovers. Most nonequal relationships fail to survive loss of exclusivity. When they do it is usually because the "errant" partner has succumbed to guilt and has been "forgiven" or "given another chance."

If you've ever had that experience, from either side, you'll know it doesn't work. Deeply felt injustice can't be willed away, and nonequal relationships are rarely, if ever, the same again. Instead of focusing on the values of the relationship, nonequal lovers allow the relationship to be lost for the sake of an ownership trip. That total loss is the ultimate cost of ownership trips and coercive monopolies.

living with equals

TO BE FREE ■ YOU MUST OFFER FREEDOM

History demonstrates that masters are as unfree as the slaves they control. Your own experience should confirm that emotional freedom can't exist for one partner in a romantic relationship if the other partner is emotionally dependent or owned.

Psychological laissez faire accepts nothing less than emotional autonomy. Unlike the old principle underlying The Myth—the practice of interference in the emotional freedom of others—psychological laissez faire celebrates the sovereignty, the autonomy, the individuality of people. Unlike the old principle, which produces relationships organized around duties, obligations, and abdications of sovereignty, psychological laissez faire produces relationships built upon continuously reaffirmed voluntarism. Unlike the old principle, which inflicts guilt on every act of freedom, psychological laissez faire rewards living free with feelings of confidence and control.

THE CONSTITUTION OF EQUALITY

Over forty years ago, Wilhelm Reich declared: "No decent person will accept love that is not given voluntarily." Since no one can actually be forced to feel love, I presume he was speaking of those who are content with accepting the rituals of love after they have become a duty.

Can love exist as a duty? If you are duty-bound can you feel self-evident love?

Equality implies voluntarism, while duties must be discharged whether you want to or not. Between equal sovereign people, every act, every expression of feeling, every commitment is voluntary and duty-free, and remains so for the life of the relationship.

I call the state of voluntarism the "I Want/You Want/ We Want" balance. *I Want* is my sovereignty. *You Want* is your sovereignty. *We Want* is where the two sovereignties mesh and transmit energy to the relationship.

Psychological laissez faire describes the limits of a relationship as identical to the limits of *We Want*. This is a dynamic and variable limitation. When two people meet and feel the attraction that prompts them to seek each other's companionship, they may have only one explicit *We Want:* to see each other again.

If and as the relationship grows, the *We Wants* grow, based on common values and needs, until a feeling of *affinity* exists in one or both for the other. Instead of experiencing the other person as a stranger, you begin to experience an affinity that creates a place in your life for that person. If you alone feel that affinity it's not a *We Want,* and your desire to escalate the relationship may have to wait. This is the pattern of growth of all relationships, platonic and romantic. They grow if the participants want them to grow; otherwise, they stagnate and die.

When platonic relationships begin to turn romantic, *I Wants* or *You Wants* may begin to replace *We Wants* as the basis of growth: the effect of The Myth. This is the point in the relationship when ownership trips may begin to develop. Advancement of the relationship may become the goal instead of individual growth, and sovereignty may become the victim.

TRIBUTARIES

Coercive romantic monopolies are not structured for growth. Nonequal lovers forget that at any given point in their lives they are the result, the sum, of the experiences they've had and how they've dealt with those experiences. You are what you value, and you create your values from your experiences and judgments.

Think of your life as a river and your experiences as tributaries of that river. Just as a river absorbs its tributaries, submerging their independent identities into its own, you absorb your experiences, the tributaries of your life. Through the judgments made, the knowledge acquired, and the values derived, you submerge the identity of these experiences into the identity of your unique life and personality.

These tributaries are not of equal importance. They contribute to your life in proportion to their size, so to speak. Profound experiences and relationships make profound contributions, and casual ones make casual contributions. Nevertheless, all tributaries are important. You are what you are because of tributaries that cover the entire range and depth of experience. Can you imagine developing deep, emotional understanding and capacity without ever having deep, emotional experiences and relationships? If your life has been shy of the profound (or shy of the casual), you will be affected by that lack sooner or later.

When you have romantic responses to someone, you are responding to your own values as they are embodied and reflected in another person who had a *particular* life with *particular* tributaries. In order to reflect and satisfy your values and needs, that person had to absorb the tributaries to their life in a way that made them a person you could love. Both partners in a romantic relationship have fashioned lives out of their own experiences that make it possible for them to have romantic responses to each other.

Coercive monopolies are destructive to lovers' tributary structures. When ownership becomes a factor in a relationship the profound tributaries begin to shrink until they eventually dry up. The kinds of profound and passionate experiences that were so important to you and your lover's development up to the day you began to evoke romantic responses from each other no longer occur. You might say, to express it in numbers, that at the start of your romantic relationship your lover had one hundred "pounds" of experience that made them a person you could love. In the course of your relationship you are "consuming" that experience through *sharing,* and if you're on an ownership trip you are consuming faster than it can be replenished by your lover's remaining tributaries. Eventually and unavoidably (under these circumstances), the one hundred pounds of experience will be totally consumed, and with it, the relationship.

This process usually underlies the complaint by one lover that the other "hasn't grown." Of course growth can't occur if the profound tributaries to your life are choked off. Instead of growth you suffer arrested development.

What *are* profound tributaries and why do they become the target of lovers on ownership trips?

Jobs, professions, or hobbies can be profound tributaries, though they are not necessarily so. They become a target for ownership trips because they are aspects of life in which the authoritarian partner may not participate to any large extent.

The most profound tributaries for most people are their *people-tributaries.* Profound people-tributaries are not necessarily romantic tributaries, but they may be. You

109

are the sum of your experiences; part of those experiences are experiences with people, and part of your experience with people is *passionate* experience with people.

Nonequal lovers are especially concerned with people-tributaries, and not only the romantic ones. People pose a far greater threat to ownership than other interests because of the (usually) greater emotional involvement present. Thus, if you're on an ownership trip you'll probably try to choke off your lover's attachment to family and friends. But your greatest effort will be to prevent your lover from having *romantic* people-tributaries.

Equal lovers take a different view. They recognize that both partners need to grow for their own sake and the sake of the relationship. Imposing limitations on growth is authoritarian. If you and your lover expose yourselves to people, if you are open to new tributaries, it is reasonable to expect some of those tributaries to become passionate in any sense of the word.

Tributaries keep you and your relationship fresh. They are the source of new material, new life experiences that replenish the values, emotions, and personality you bring to your lover and the relationship you share.

SEX ROLES

Conventional sex roles serve to lock men and women into the approved monogamous life-style. The general pattern confines women to the management of the family unit and men to the unit's support. This organization tends to focus the couple's attention on the family unit as an end in itself, as opposed to such a unit being considered a by-product of the romantic choices of two sovereign individuals.

I don't mean to imply that most couples enter into marriage (or other forms of exclusive cohabitational relationships) solely for the purpose of establishing families and without romantic emotions between them. Certainly romantic emotions are the starting point of the whole process. What I do mean, however, is that the *a priori* acceptance of The Myth's family-unit life-style often results in elevating the value of that unit *over* the value of emotional freedom as if the two were incompatible.

The Myth urges women to give up emotional freedom for housekeeping and motherhood in exchange for financial, social, sexual, and physical security. It persuades men to give up the same freedom for the role of financial, social, sexual, and physical protector in exchange for a domestic major domo. For both partners the "rewards" for accepting these roles are the "old-time religion" of family satisfactions and the assurance of regular, convenient and presumably agreeable sex.

These tradeoffs are fundamental to society's attempt to control sexual behavior. Sex becomes a "reward" for compliance with society's roles instead of being the natural and rewarding result of a healthy, sovereign emotional freedom.

111

The American culture, in particular, is accused of being both sexually uptight and obsessed with sex. As often noted, these two states of mind are logically connected. After all, considering the actual importance of sexuality in human experience one would expect obsession to follow prohibition. It should also be noted (if it hasn't been) that the approved exclusive, family-unit life-style contributes to that uptight, obsessive condition. The abdication of sovereignty always extracts a price, and the imposition and acceptance of sex roles is no exception.

Historically, the monogamous family-unit life-style, originated and enforced by male-dominated societies, has made chattels of women. Until recently, women's sovereignty has not only been ignored, but for the most part its existence has been denied. Women were considered inferior beings in most physical, psychological, legal, and even moral respects. Menstruation was shameful and unclean. Female sexual desire was unholy—extramarital romances were the result of witches' power over their lovers. Women were (and often still are) considered flighty, irrational, undependable, emotionally unstable, ad infinitum. In short, women were considered the rightful chattels of their menfolk—when they weren't considered outright evil—because they were incompetent in all but domestic concerns.

The destruction of women's sovereignty extracted a price from both sexes, a subject examined more thoroughly in feminist literature than is possible here. One outstanding result is the sexual double standard. Since women were chattels, men had to assume the obligations and restrictions of the role of owner and protector. This stripped men of their emotional sovereignty as surely as it was stripped from women. From their position of power, however, men could engage in covert exercise of emotional freedom. Unfortunately (and, with the benefit of hindsight, not surprisingly), the covert nature of that exercise of freedom often dehumanized and immoralized the results. As a consequence, the double standard institutionalized deceit and lack of openness between "legal" romantic partners; a condition that is almost as prevalent today as it was in the past. It is, moreover, an important factor in our culture's sexual obsession.

The double standard is a two-edged piece of mischief. Devised as half a safety valve to make compulsory monogamy tolerable (at least for men), it has succeeded in seriously undermining what it was intended to preserve. Originally it encouraged sexual independence in men (although covertly expressed), but women are now assuming the same prerogative. The result is a growing acceptance of sexual independence prior to marriage that society expects both men and women to abandon after marriage—an irrational expectation. The inevitable result must be (sorry, Myth) continually growing sexual independence that is antithetical to monogamy.

In response to chattelization, women had to devise means for experiencing some control over their lives—and men grudgingly recognized that women should be allowed to do so. Since women were effectively prevented from exercising this control as totally sovereign individuals, they developed forms of control within their domestic status. For example, women usually run their homes relatively free from male interference.

One kind of control, a by-product of the way the conjugal relationship was structured by men, produced a set of sex roles particularly damaging to sovereignty. These are the supplicant/bestower roles. Traditionally, men have been the initiators of sex and women the responders. In the past, male initiation took the form of a demand, explicitly or implicitly. Female response was limited to compliance, although women could convey a preference for refusal by appealing to health or simply by being detached and uninvolved while complying.

Today, it is brutish (but not unheard of) for men to demand sex from their partners. In order to initiate they either simply ask or communicate their desire by more subtle means. In any event, the responsibility for sexual initiation remains, by and large, with the male.

One question I asked each of my lecture audiences was whether the men had ever been in a relationship where their lovers had initiated sex as often, or more often, than they. The affirmative responses were always negligible. Equally negligible were affirmative answers from women to the question of whether they usually or often initiated sex. Moreover, when I asked the men what their reaction would be if their lovers were sexually assertive, the response was enthusiastic. On the other hand, when I asked the women what they thought about sexually assertive females, the response was basically negative, although often somewhat tinged with wistful envy.

Obviously, these answers indicate a possible mismatch between men and women on the issue of sexual initiation, and if you think about it, this is not surprising.

Most of the men I've questioned on this issue have not been happy about always having to be the initiators. I've asked them if over a long period of time that role has given them the feeling of being *supplicants,* and almost without exception, their response has been a resounding "Yes!"

Think about that. Our culturally induced sex roles make men feel like supplicants—beggars for the highest expression of the relationship they share with their partners.

This absurd role pattern—man as the supplicant and woman as the bestower—undercuts both partners' sovereignty. For the man the reason is obvious: One who must beg, and who is dependent on another for the realization of their values, can't feel sovereign and independent. But the woman's sovereignty is undercut as well: As the bestower, she is also a responder. That is, if she doesn't initiate, she must wait for the man to initiate before she can respond. If he doesn't initiate, she has nothing to respond to and thus loses control over the expression of her own sexual desires.

Now, in all the foregoing I don't mean to imply that no women ever engage in any kind of sexual initiation, although in the recent past that may have been close to accurate. Nevertheless, I believe that, by and large, in most relationships the responsibility for initiation falls more heavily on the man than on the woman. This pair of sex roles undercuts the sovereignty and diminishes the viability of any romantic relationship because of the potential for misunderstanding and resentment. Eventually, the man whose partner is a noninitiator will begin to wonder if the partner is still sexually interested—and there goes his visibility, both sexual and psychological. If he decides to stop initiating in the hope that his partner will start, she may well misunderstand and believe that he has lost interest in her. This kind of cycle inevitably breeds resentment; if not checked, it will destroy a relationship.

This pair of sex roles is the source of another problem. No one enjoys being rejected, especially sexually. When bestower/supplicant roles are part of a relationship, rejection may easily follow. For the supplicant, each time his partner is disinterested in sex it can be misunderstood as "another" example of a basic lack of sexual interest in him. ("Another" example added to the belief that since she *never* initiates, she couldn't be very interested in the first place.) For the bestower, sensitive to the possibility of causing feelings of rejection, there may be a tendency to engage in sex even if not inclined. This amounts to charity for him and duty for her, and if they were both consciously aware of it they'd be horrified.

Equal lovers don't have this problem because they both initiate sex. As a result, neither lacks for evidence that the other is sexually interested, nor are they bothered with feelings of rejection if the other prefers a good book to sex on occasion. After all, it's pretty hard to feel rejected tonight if your lover initiated lovemaking last night or the night before. By getting rid of the supplicant/bestower roles it is manifestly clear that in general *I Want* and *You Want* sex with each other and when those two *Wants* become a *We Want,* light the candles.

When they don't, there was last night and tomorrow night and no hurt feelings in between.

LIVING WITH EQUALS

Living with equals means giving up your authoritarianism and adopting the principle of psychological laissez faire.

If you've decided to opt for equality you'll discover there's no easy way to rearrange your life. There's no magic wand that with a mere wave will turn an unequal relationship into an equal one. You'll need patience and determination. Treating people as sovereign equals is sometimes disturbing, but you'll be surprised how quickly most people will get used to it.

There are two kinds of problems we are likely to encounter, of which the first is our own fears. The foremost fear will be of *uncertainty*. We've had the comfort of The Myth all our lives, and if it hasn't worked, it has at least provided a goal. Now, at the crossroads, we've decided against "resignation" and "adjustment" in favor of our own direction. Uncertainty is to be expected. Don't fight it, use it. The unexpected, even when it's the result of false starts and mistakes, provides material to grow on.

A more personally troubling fear may result from your own benevolence and goodwill: the fear of causing un-

117

happiness in others. This is particularly true if you're now in an unequal romantic relationship. Whichever side of the inequality you're on, you'll probably be concerned about the possible unhappiness your lover may experience as a result of your insistence on equality. That is a legitimate concern. After all, you have also contributed to the inequality, and there are consequences of that contribution you must face.

If you are the one who has been on the ownership trip your lover may have come to depend on that. If he or she is not prepared to reassert sovereignty, sudden independence may be a shock. It's a delicate situation that requires much patience, but be wary: It can also be a trap. A subtle kind of emotional blackmail can occur in this situation that capitalizes on concern and benevolence. This is the Final Appeal.

Jess and Arthur had been married about five years when Jess began to question the basis of their marriage. At the time, Jess wasn't thinking in terms of sovereignty and ownership trips, but she knew that she was the stronger of the two in certain ways and that Arthur had become quite dependent. She was even aware of capitalizing on that dependence from time to time, and it angered her to do so.

For over a year Jess tried to rearrange the relationship. She told Arthur that she was afraid his dependence was hurting the marriage, and he seemed to be trying to work out of it. But at every crucial point his dependence would return. Jess felt more and more suffocated as time passed.

Just before reaching the all but inevitable breaking point, they had a terrible row. "Arthur," Jess cried, "can't you see you've given up your own life? I don't want to carry the load for both of us."

Arthur's answer was, "Jessica, that's the way I am. Why can't you accept me as I am? Why must you try to change me? Do your thing and let me do mine. I depend on you because I love and respect you. Is that so bad?"

Jessica was stunned. She realized that she wanted to be accepted as the person *she* was, but she wasn't willing to accept Arthur. And he did love her, no question about that. Maybe, she thought, she was being unreasonable.

So she tried, she really tried. But it didn't do any good. For a while she thought the problem was all hers. And then it occurred to her that there was more to it than that. As she told me later, "I realized that Art was saying, 'Jess, I love you, and because I do you should love me back even if I'm not quite what you want me to be.'

"But that's not fair. Sure I should accept him, as a person, the way he is, but that doesn't mean I'm obligated to love that person. He's changed since we've been married, and if I met him now for the first time I wouldn't love him. I can't fake it and I'm not going to try."

119

Jess was right. Arthur wasn't consciously trying to black-mail Jess, but that is always the effect of the Final Appeal.

Be benevolent, but don't let it trap you.

Another fear you may encounter is fear of being *secondary*. Equal relationships aren't always natural monopolies. Your lover may have another relationship and it might be *primary*. It's a good deal easier to handle the idea of your lover having a relationship with someone else if you know that you're number one. But what if you're not?

First, what do *primary* and *secondary* mean? All relationships are primary in the respect that you are loved for what you are. The values that attract your lover's romantic responses are of primary importance to them. In that respect the relationship is primary—it exists for unique reasons.

A relationship may be considered secondary only in the respects of emotional importance or allotment of time—and the latter is usually proportional to the former. If your lover has a relationship of greater emotional importance than the relationship with you, you may reasonably describe your relationship as secondary in that respect. However, the relationship is still primary on the basis of its emotional importance to you, and it is primary in the respect that you are loved for the unique person you are.

Your ability to handle being secondary is one of the acid tests of your own sovereignty. It comes down to this: You love someone; that's the reality of your life. Because of your values and their values, you love that person. Now, how about the reality of your lover's life? Can you be nonauthoritarian enough to handle that?

The reality of that person's life is: Besides loving you, your lover also loves someone else and that *other* relationship is primary. This is a test of *your* sovereignty, because you are faced with one pro- and one anti-sovereignty choice. The anti-sovereignty choice is: "To hell with my values, the values that cause me to love that person and to hell with that person's values too. The most important value to me is that I have that person all to myself. That's the highest value on *my* romantic hierarchy."

The pro-sovereignty choice is: "Because of my values and their values, I love that person and I don't turn away from my values just because I can't achieve them totally (or for any other reason, either). Besides, by being nonauthoritarian, the relationship will still exist when and if I'm ever in the position to achieve them totally."

Unlike the courtly game of medieval times, being secondary isn't necessarily forever; nor does it confine you to the shelf between times as happens to the mistress of a lover who is a captive of The Myth. (Male "mistresses" haven't bought the "shelf" idea, for the most part.)

You know what you want out of your romantic relationships. If you get it, being secondary really shouldn't matter.

EQUAL LIFE-STYLES

Psychological laissez faire has strong implications for life-styles. Any life-style that interferes with emotional freedom can't be laissez faire. Some life-styles are more conducive to ownership trips than others, but whether or not authoritarianism enters a relationship ultimately depends on the people involved. Still, the susceptibility is real and needs to be dealt with.

Obviously, the life-style most conducive to ownership trips is the coercive monopoly marriage since it is based on ownership in the first place. But, setting aside the issue of marriage itself for now, the fundamental life-style question for sovereign and autonomous people is: to live with or apart from your lover.

If you are now living with a lover, or ever have, think back to the point in that relationship when you were *on the verge* of thinking about living together. The relationship was probably at its peak in excitement and satisfaction. (It may still be, but it almost certainly was then.) Both of you had lives separate from the other, regardless of how large your common life was.

In the separate portion of your lives you were (or should have been) completely free and uninhibited in continuing to grow and develop tributaries. You were financially independent. Your relationship was voluntary; you knew that the time you spent together was the result of making that choice over other alternatives.

With all that, you were still (probably) "living together" a great deal of the time. You just weren't sharing a mailbox; that is, you had to go home once in a while to pick up your mail at least. During that phase of living together there probably was a degree of back-and-forthness to your cohabitation if you each had your own home or apartment.

Now all these conditions inhibit ownership trips and support sovereignty. Because of the degree of separateness in your lives, both of you could continue to grow. Tributaries, including people-tributaries, expanded; your financial independence protected your sovereignty; the voluntarism in the situation discouraged ownership trips because you were both free to make other arrangements if either of you began to crowd the other. Even the influence of competition helped prevent ownership trips because you were in no position to take your lover for granted or place any arbitrary expectations on them.

Having separate places to live is especially effective in discouraging ownership trips. If you have your own space, even if you're not often there, *you have a place to go*. It's a reasonable assumption that, since it's *your space,* you'll choose to be in it once in a while (and more often than that if you have to fight off your lover's ownership attempts).

All these advantages may disappear once you begin sharing a mailbox. (*May,* I said. Remember, life-styles may or may not produce problems, depending on the people.) Proximity may inhibit separateness. Growth and tributaries may suffer. Certainly financial *inter*dependence can easily become financial dependence. And if you are sharing a mailbox, where do you go to be *really* alone or do your own private thing? Home to mother?

Again, I want to emphasize that not every cohabitative relationship has these problems—only the majority of them do, at least after several years. It's also true that the arguments *for* mailbox sharing are persuasive: Two incomes are better than one, and one rent is better than two; it's nice to cut down on phone bills and the transportation back and forth between spaces; it's nice to know *for sure* what you're going to be doing Saturday night, and it's nice to have someone around who knows where you are all the time. (Aren't those last two items a little suspicious?)

Remember that living apart doesn't preclude living together as much as you wish. It merely makes it easier to live apart as much as your independence and sovereignty require.

Ronald Mazur observed that "people who refuse to risk spacing end separating." After a generation of "togetherness," people are beginning to understand the importance of psychic space. I hope they'll also begin to appreciate physical space; not just the privacy provided by a closed door, but the separateness you get from being truly *away* from the people who share most of the days of your life.

Separateness is a fact and a blessing. It's the source of autonomy. When people lose their sense of separateness they begin to feel like anonymous parts of a machine, replaceable by any one of a million available spares. It happens all the time in romantic relationships, this feeling that you are a *function* not a *person*. Spacing is the antidote. New people and new experiences help replenish your substance, and when you share those new things with the people who share most of the days of your life, you add substance to those relationships.

Marriage is mailbox sharing and all the above applies; but if you're already married, the situation is more complex. Married or unmarried, if you and your lover are living under the same roof and intend to have an equal relationship, you will have to structure things to fit your special circumstances and needs.

One couple I know, of modest means, feel they can't afford two apartments, but they also feel they can't afford to do without some private and independent living on their own. One technique they've adopted is to budget $25 a week ($1300 per year) for an escape fund. That provides $650 per year for each for getting away. They don't ask each other's permission, they just go. It's not much, but it's something.

According to statistics, marriage isn't doing well lately. Regardless, many people studying the subject predict that marriage is here to stay. Considering its long history, that may be so; but monarchy had a long history, too, and look what's happened to it. In the end, marriage is irrelevant to living with equals. I'm not sure that marriage—unofficial if possible, official if necessary—can add anything to a truly equal relationship; but if it can for you, you will be happier for having added it. I am sure that for some people official marriage can detract from an equal relationship, and the implication of that is obvious.

"Marriage" is a relationship more than a ceremony, and considering society's authoritarian interference in the decisions of husbands and wives to end their marriages, I believe the ceremony should be boycotted. Not everyone agrees.

The most potent argument defending marriage involves children. One of the threats used to support society's efforts to control sexual behavior is the punishment of children for the independence and autonomy of their parents. This is a tactic appropriate for a bully and hence for authoritarian society. The epitome of this obscenity is the concept "bastardy." How can there be an *illegitimate child?* Questions of inheritance and such are not really the issue; they can be settled other ways. The classification "illegitimate" means more in this society than who gets a cut of the estate. The concept of illegitimacy, or bastardy, is an abomination that deserves to be quickly dispatched.

Beyond that, divorced single parents have always had to reconcile their independent, unmated life-styles with parenthood. There is nothing new I can say on the subject. Instead, read what Mary has to say:

*　*　*

"I'm raising David with complete respect for his autonomy. Often I know that a person in the room with us is thinking, 'Why doesn't she tell that child to shut up?' I have literally thrown men out of the house who have tried to assume a father role they had no right to assume. Also, I have always been very cautious in dealing with my romantic relationships as far as David is concerned. A child between the ages of one and ten has a condensed viewpoint, and I didn't want him to have breakfast with many different 'uncles' and get the idea that sex is very casual. My relationship with Phil has gone on for two years. At what time I'm going to say, 'This is really a permanent relationship, and I think it's okay for us to be openly together,' I don't know. I just don't want David to think that sex is just something that is promiscuous and casual.

"I have said to him there may someday be a 'real' family, if I choose to get married again; a third party will be involved. He has expressed a negative attitude about that and I've informed him that it really wasn't any of his business. I've said, 'Look, David, you'll probably leave when you're nineteen and I'll be by myself, so it really doesn't concern you.' He accepts that."

There's another argument for marriage. It's couched in many different terms, but they all boil down to the same thing: fear. The following is from a conversation I had with Penny about her friend Bill:

* * *

127

PENNY: Bill and I have a running argument about marriage. I don't think marriage has to be binding and I can't see myself being married to someone who doesn't want to have other relationships. But I am a rather private person. I don't go around broadcasting what I believe in. If two people live together, they stand out. If they go through formal marriage they get the approval of society and what goes on within your household is another matter.

JK: You're putting up society as a standard for your actions, your life. Why not just say you're married and use Bill's name?

PENNY: That's dishonest if we're not married. It denotes a relationship that doesn't exist really.

JK: What about a wife who doesn't take her husband's name? Is that dishonest?

PENNY: No. She has that right.

JK: Well, on the issue of privacy I think you are as justified in saying you're married when you're not as in saying what goes on in your household is nobody's business.

PENNY: I can't agree with you. I really feel that would be a compromise on principles. If you're going to be lovers and flaunt society, I can't see taking what I consider half measures. Just go so far, then say, "We'll take all the good things and just put up a front and say we're married." By living together there is still a stigma attached, especially for a woman. You can be hurt by people that you care about and who don't understand what's going on in your head. Marriage seems to placate them without com-

128

promising yourself. Formal marriage is nothing. It's just going to a justice of the peace and saying, "I do." It's placating everyone and you're not compromising yourself.

JK: Doing it is nothing, but the consequences are not nothing. That strikes me as being the ultimate compromise of principles.

PENNY: I think it's just as bad to tell people, "Hey, we're living in sin." It's just as bad.

"Flaunt society," "take all the good things and just put up a front," "stigma," "placate them," and the ever-popular "living in sin"—these are the phrases of abdication. Penny is deeply concerned about being judged harshly by society. She would rather fake the public commitment of marriage than have society realize that she considers marriage a "nothing."

Since she can't see herself "being married to someone who doesn't want to have other relationships"—as she made clear to me *she* wants—Penny seems prepared to be viewed by society as an "unfaithful" wife. This makes one wonder why she considers being "unfaithful" a lesser stigma than being independent of society's romantic Myth.

Whether we are married or not, living together or apart, with or without children, the fundamentals of equality are the same. Sovereignty and psychological laissez faire offer a greater number of specific life-style options than any one person can imagine. The Myth offers only one.

No other person, legal arbiter, social tradition, or system of morality can surpass the effectiveness of your own values in deciding what constitutes happiness for you. Your particular genius in this decision rests in the fact that you are the only one who knows for a certainty just what *your* happiness is. Use that genius to develop your own options—to build your own road.

Sovereign and autonomous people are impossible to pigeonhole. The very fact that they are self-defining means that only *they* can tell you what they value, hence what they are. But I believe all sovereign people will agree that a romantic relationship based on equality and psychological laissez faire must include *the emotional freedom to give everything to your lover and the relationship without being concerned that the gift will be used in an attempt to restrict your freedom.*

That is living with equals.

glossary

Authoritarianism: The doctrine of obedience to authority as opposed to individual liberty.

Commitment: A pledge, usually of sexual exclusivity.

Differences, corroding: Value or personality differences that eat away at a relationship and often become terminal.

Differences, growth: Differences between lovers that each uses for personal growth.

Differences, terminal: Differences that are so fundamentally important that they cause the end of a romantic relationship.

Emotion: The automated psychosomatic response to some aspect of reality based on prior value judgments.

Emotional blackmail: The attempt to manipulate someone into agreement, usually through the instilling of guilt.

Envy: The emotional response to the experience of recognizing values you desire and do not yet have.

Final appeal: A form of emotional blackmail that capitalizes on benevolence and the desire to avoid causing pain to others.

Hierarchy of values: The conscious or subconscious arranging of a person's values by order of importance.

Insecurity: The emotional response to the experience of fearfulness over your ability to achieve or retain your values.

I Want/You Want/We Want balance: An expression of the relationship between the separate sovereignties of two lovers and the meshing of those sovereignties.

Jealousy: The emotional response to the loss or threat of loss of emotional property.

Mailbox sharing: Romantic cohabitation.

Ownership, emotional: The power to control, define, and/or inhibit the values, actions, goals, thoughts, and convictions of another; the control of any or all aspects of another person's life.

Poacher/predator mentality: The proprietary attitude toward a lover marked by the belief that your lover is your property and that anyone who gains value from that property is a thief, that the world is populated by such thieves intent on stealing your property, and that your lover is powerless to resist those thieves.

Psychological laissez faire: Noninterference in the emotional freedom of others.

Psychosomatic: Physical states or changes produced by psychological stimuli.

Romance-values: The values a person holds which govern romantic choices. *Positive romance-values* are supportive of sovereignty. *Negative romance-values* undercut sovereignty. *Cultural romance-values* are those promoted by cultural standards. *Stereotyped romance-values* are based on preconceived notions. *Transient romance-values* are those based on temporary conditions.

Romantic monopolies: Exclusive romantic relationships. *Coercive romantic monopolies* are exclusive by prior and binding agreement, and *natural romantic monopolies* are not.

Romantic relationship: An intimate personal relationship based on values. Nonplatonic love.

Sense of loss: A real or imagined emotional response to the involuntary ending of a romantic relationship.

Separateness: The absolute individuality of a person relative to others.

Sexual visibility: The experience of having your sexual identity perceived by others as you yourself perceive it.

Shared values: Close correspondence of values, especially between lovers.

Siege component: The aspect of jealousy implying that your lover is defenseless against predators.

Sovereignty: The independent prerogative to determine your own values, actions, goals, thoughts, and convictions.

Spacing: The need or impulse for being physically or psychically apart from others, including lovers; more than just the privacy of having "a room of your own."

Supplicant/bestower: Sex roles in which one partner

characteristically initiates sex and the other merely responds.

Tabula rasa: "Blank tablet." The preknowledge state of infant consciousness.

Theft component: The aspect of jealousy implying that loss of a lover's affection, attention, or time is an injustice committed against you.

Tributaries: The experiences in your life about which you make the value judgments that define you as an individual.

Value: That which one acts to gain or keep. Values vary in importance. *High values* are those you consider important to your life. *Low values* are those considered only marginally important. *Nonvalues* are those considered irrelevant. *Disvalues* are those considered harmful to your life.

Value conflict: The clash between two mutually exclusive values.

Value judgment: The perception of an aspect of reality as either a value or a disvalue.

Visibility: The experience of being perceived by others in the same way in which you perceive yourself. Having your own self-estimate confirmed by the way other people act toward you.

Volition: Free will; the capacity to choose between alternatives.

acknowledgments

As others who have acknowledged the important influences in their intellectual lives, I want to register the debt of gratitude I feel toward those whose work has contributed to my own. Among these are Ayn Rand, Edith Efron, Nathaniel Branden, Abraham Maslow, Murray Rothbard, Henry Hazlitt, Robert A. Heinlein, Betty Friedan, Germaine Greer, Harry Browne, and the many libertarians whose friendship is both intellectually and personally important to me.

During the two years of this project my spirit was sustained by dozens of people, friends and strangers (no longer, I hope). In particular I am indebted to Judith and Ken Costello, who first suggested that others might be interested in these ideas; psychologist Sharon Presley,

135

whose encouragement and assistance in the first months was valuable beyond measure. (I hope she is pleased with the results.) Also to Bill Lawry, Ann Weil, and Ray Strong for their continuing help and encouragement; to Oscar Collier and editor Eleanor Friede for their confidence and enthusiasm; to those wonderfully articulate people who attended my lectures and the long-suffering interviewees; and by no means least, to Jill Angelique Maria Teresa St. Ambrogio for months of brainstorming in the beginning, steel-willed production at the end, and tea and sympathy in between.

bibliography

ARNOLD, MAGDA. *Emotion and Personality*. New York: Columbia University Press, 1960.

BERNE, ERIC. *Games People Play*. New York: Grove Press, 1964. Paperback, Ballantine, 1974.

BRANDEN, NATHANIEL. *The Psychology of Self-Esteem*. Los Angeles: Nash Publishing, 1969. Paperback, Bantam, 1971.

CONSTANTINE, LARRY L. and JOAN M. *Group Marriage: A Study of Contemporary Multilateral Marriage*. New York: Macmillan, 1973. Paperback, Collier, 1974.

HARRIS, THOMAS. *I'm OK—You're OK: A Practical Guide to Transactional Analysis*. New York: Harper & Row, 1969. Paperback, Avon, 1973.

HEINLEIN, ROBERT A. *Stranger in a Strange Land*. New York: Putnam, 1961. Paperback, Berkley, 1975.

———. *Time Enough for Love*. New York: Putnam, 1973. Paperback, Berkley, 1974.

———. *Glory Road.* New York: Berkley (paperback), 1970.

JAMES, MURIEL, and JONGEWARD, DOROTHY. *Born to Win: Transactional Analysis with Gestalt Experiments.* Reading, Mass.: Addison-Wesley, 1971. Paperback, Addison-Wesley, 1972.

MASLOW, ABRAHAM. *Toward a Psychology of Being.* New York: Van Nostrand Reinhold, 1968. Paperback, Van Nostrand Reinhold, 1968.

———. *The Farther Reaches of Human Nature.* Big Sur, Calif.: Esalen Institute, 1971. Paperback, Viking, 1972.

MAZUR, RONALD. *The New Intimacy: Open Ended Marriage and Alternative Life-Style.* Boston: Beacon Press, 1973. Paperback, Beacon Press, 1974.

O'NEILL, NENA and GEORGE. *Open Marriage: A New Life-Style for Couples.* New York: M. Evans, 1972. Paperback, Avon, 1973.

RAND, AYN. *The Virtue of Selfishness.* New York: Norton, 1964. Paperback, New American Library, 1964.

———. *Anthem.* Caldwell, Idaho: Caxton, 1966. Paperback, New American Library, 1961.

ROGERS, CARL. *Becoming Partners.* New York: Delacorte Press, 1972. Paperback, Dell, 1973.

———. *Person to Person: The Problem of Being Human.* Lafayette, Calif.: Real People, 1967. Paperback, Pocket, 1975.

STEVENS, JOHN. *Awareness: Exploring, Experimenting, Experiencing.* Lafayette, Calif.: Real People, 1971. Paperback, Bantam, 1973.

WILLIAMS, ROGER, JR. *You Are Extraordinary.* New York: Random House, 1967. Paperback, Pyramid, 1971.

index

Aristotle, 49

Authoritarianism, 18–20

Bisexuality, 78

Branden, Nathaniel, 17, 49, 54

Coercive Romantic Monopolies, 88–100; definition, 88, 100; three arguments for, 89–98; 100% Rule, 90–92; lasting commitment, 93–96; Sharing, 96–98; comparisons, 97–98; effects of, 99–100; and efficacy, 99–100; and loss of control, 100 (See also Tributaries)

Differences, 25–29; corroding, growth and terminal, 27–28

Emotion, 47–73; definition, 49; changing emotional patterns, 67–73; checklist, 71–73

Emotional blackmail, 22–24

Emotional property (See Jealousy)

Emotional visibility (See Romance-values)

Envy, cf Jealousy; definition, 32; and covetousness, 32

Equality, 9–10, 24–25

Expectations, unfulfilled 24–25

Final Appeal, 118–120

139

Hierarchy of values, 47–73, 60–67; High-, low-, non- and disvalues, 61–66; analyzing, 62–67; sample, 65–67
Homosexuality, 78
"I Want/You Want/We Want" balance, 106–107
Incest taboo, 78
Insecurity, cf Jealousy; definition, 32
Jealousy, 30–46; compared to envy and insecurity, 31–35; definition, 33; and emotional property, 33; and loss, 33–34; and ownership, 35; poacher/ predator mentality, 36–38, 39; theft and siege components of, 38–39, 40; as unavoidable, 40–42; as productive, 42; cure for, 43–44; and openness, 44–46
Life-styles: monogamous family unit, 112; double-standard, 112–113; mailbox-sharing (cohabitation) 124–134; marriage, 125–126; parenthood, 126–127; and sovereignty, 127–129
Living with equals: checklist, 14, 25, 105–130; and uncertainty, 117
Love, 74–86; self-evident nature of, 75–77; nonromantic, 76; romantic, 76–78; and sovereignty, 77; and values, 86 (See also Romantic responses, differentiating)
Marriage, (See life-styles, sovereignty)
Mazur, Ronald, 124
Monogamy, 89
Monopolies, Romantic: definition, 88
Myth, The, ix, 6–7, 21, 77, 88, 89–90, 105
Natural Romantic Monopolies: definition, 101; compared to coercive romantic monopolies, 101–102; and exclusivity, 102–103; and periodicity, 103
Openness (See Jealousy)
Options, 8–9
Ownership: definition, 20; 20, 21, 25, 30 (See also Jealousy)
Poacher/Predator mentality (See Jealousy)
Psychological laissez-faire: definition, 87; 105–106
Rand, Ayn, 3, 51
Reich, Wilhelm, 106
Romance-values, 53–60; emotional visibility, 53–56; shared values, 56–57; sexual visibility, 57–58; and sovereignty, 58–60; positive, 58–59; negative, 58–59; cultural, 59–60; stereotype, 60; obscure, 66–67; transient, 80
Romantic relationships,

primary and secondary,
120–122
Romantic responses,
differentiating: and
romantic hierarchy, 79–80;
and strength of response,
80–81; and transient
values, 80; scales of
measurement, 79–86; and
rarely-met values, 80; sense
of loss, 83–86
Sex roles, 110–116;
supplicant/bestower,
114–117
Sexual visibility (see
Romance-values)
Shared values (See *Romance
values*)
Siege component (See
Jealousy)
Sovereignty, 9–10, 15–29;
definition, 16; and love,

77; 85 (See also *coercive
monopoly, natural
monopoly and
romance-values*)
Spacing, need for physical
124–125
Standards, personal 12–13
Tabula rasa, 6
Theft component (See
Jealousy)
Tributaries: definition, 107;
107–110; and coercive
monopolies, 108–109;
people tributaries, 109–110
Values, 9–10, 25, 47–73;
definition, 51; integrating,
52; hidden, 63–64 (See
also *Hierarchies* and
Romance-values)
Value judgments, 49–50
Volition, 16
Voluntarism, 88–89, 106